The F

The Hour is Come

Passion in Real Time

Andrew Nunn

CANTERBURY
PRESS
Norwich

© Andrew Nunn 2021

First published in 2021 by the Canterbury Press Norwich
Editorial office
3rd Floor, Invicta House
108–114 Golden Lane
London EC1Y 0TG, UK

www.canterburypress.co.uk

Canterbury Press is an imprint of Hymns Ancient & Modern Ltd
(a registered charity)

Hymns Ancient & Modern® is a registered trademark of
Hymns Ancient & Modern Ltd
13A Hellesdon Park Road, Norwich,
Norfolk NR6 5DR, UK

British Library Cataloguing in Publication data

A catalogue record for this book is available
from the British Library

978 1-78622-396-8

Typeset by Regent Typesetting
Printed and bound in Great Britain by
CPI Group (UK) Ltd

Contents

Preface

Although by birth and inclination I am a city person – I was born in Leicester and have worked in Leeds and London – I have never been in such a fast-moving place as I am at the moment. Being the Dean of Southwark means that you have the joy and the responsibility of living in the Deanery, a house which stands on Bankside, on the south side of the Thames, in between the Globe Theatre and Tate Modern and opposite St Paul's Cathedral. There is not a moment when there is not something happening outside or on the river. Joggers, walkers, strollers make their way past the house all the time. To be honest I don't mind that at all; it gives me energy and a sense of being in the midst of things that are happening.

Similarly the cathedral in which I have been ministering since 1999 is right in the thick of things. Southwark Cathedral, for those unfamiliar with London, is set alongside London Bridge and is surrounded by railway lines and the busy Borough Market. For most of its long history – well over a thousand years – it has looked down on its neighbours, it being the tallest and most prominent building in the area. Now it is dwarfed by the Shard and by most other buildings that are constructed as the City of London makes its way south of the river.

One of those neighbours is the News Building, the home of *The Times* and *The Sun* and many other publications. The lights are always on as the business of collecting and curating news happens all day, every day. It's a great feeling to be in this buzzing, busy environment. Not for us the green grass of an ancient cathedral close but the gritty reality and the glorious joy and positivity of the city. It's a place in which life is comfortable for some and a struggle for others, in which a few are living in multi-million-pound apartments, others are in more modest public housing, and others are trying to keep safe and dry in doorways. The contrasts could not be more extreme.

But there is the cathedral, a constant presence, something of a calm oasis in a desperately busy world, and a place where people try to make sense of what is going on in their lives. As a consequence of not charging for admission, some people wander in to light a candle, to stand and stare, to see if they can spot the cathedral cat, first the famous Doorkins, now Hodge, to catch up with our Shakespeare connections, or simply to see what the inside of the building looks like. Frankly I don't care why they come in, I'm just pleased that they do come in. If, while they are with us, they can catch just a glimpse, a hint of God in the midst of their own lives, then we have done something for them.

Southwark Cathedral has a reputation, derived from the 1960s theological movement named 'South Bank Religion' and from the legacy of John Robinson's famous book *Honest to God*, of being a place that doesn't shy away from theology. I wouldn't class myself as any kind of academic theologian but what I have done in just under forty years of ordained ministry is to try to understand how theology connects with life. Being a priest in a church sandwiched between roads and river, railway and market, means that you have ample opportunities to do that and to work out what we mean when we talk of the doctrine of the incarnation.

It is out of all of this that I pray and write. Since 2012 I have written a daily Twitter prayer, responding to the psalmody for the day and hopefully articulating something of what others might be wanting to say to God. For the same amount of time I have been writing a weekly blog, 'Living God', an opportunity for me to share my thoughts but also to encourage other people to make the connections between life and faith and the living God. So whether the issues are around Brexit or Trump, around sexuality or race, around cats or cleaning, I have tried to see what the Bible has to say to us, what poets have to say to us, what popular culture has to say to us, what life has to say to us, and offer all that in reflection and prayer.

That is where this book fits in. Born of a desire to set the events of the Passion into the context of the fast-paced, news-hungry, hard reality of the city, to get the pace of the story and the urgency of the Gospels into our thinking, and out of my own love for Jerusalem and the Via Dolorosa, I embarked on this journey, in real time. I hope you enjoy the journey.

Andrew Nunn

Introduction

We live in a world in which news is available at every moment, in real time, constantly updated. This is what we have come to expect – the 'Breaking News' banner at the bottom of the screen updating us on the very latest developments in a story. Whether this is good for us I don't know, but it is the world in which we live. It was this reality that made me think again about the reality that the writers of the Gospels draw us into in Holy Week. Most of what they write has no fixings in time; we don't know quite when Jesus was in Capernaum, when he encountered the widow in Nain, when he called his disciples, what day of the week he told the parable of the sower. But Holy Week is very different.

The pace of each of the gospel accounts changes and we are given so much more detail of what and when things happen, even down to precise timings – '*It was nine o'clock in the morning when they crucified him*' (Mark 15.25). The order of events may vary slightly but on most things most of the writers are agreed.

The practice of the church has been to immerse us in the accounts of the Passion. On Palm Sunday we read one of the three synoptic accounts, Matthew, Mark or Luke. On Good Friday it is always John that we read. So every year we hear the story from two perspectives and through dramatic presentation, through the singing of the Passion, we are drawn into the reality and the emotion and the passion of the Passion.

I once had a colleague at Southwark Cathedral who used to be incensed at the way in which the church treats the birth narratives. I can hear him now complaining about the much-loved service of Nine Lessons and Carols, and how the smashing together of Matthew's and Luke's very different accounts of the birth of Jesus was an abuse of scripture and revealed a shocking ignorance. Though his complaints fell on deaf ears (we continued to mix up shepherds and magi), what he said did stay with me. So I do apologize to all those biblical scholars who will wince at what I have done in this book.

At the same time, I think when we are wishing to enter into the experience of Jesus and his disciples and all the other players in Holy Week, it is a good thing to immerse ourselves in the story, and using the concept of 'real time' helps us to do this.

As I get older I find that the historical Jesus, the incarnate Jesus, the God who enters real time, my real time, becomes more important to me. The concept of the God of all time who enters our time, the God who exists in eternity subjecting the divine self to what it means to be human and to be the participant in unfolding time with all its implications, thrills me and fires my spirit. We do not believe in a distant God, out there, detached, but a God so intimately involved that the ticking clock becomes part of how we know Jesus.

This book and this journey begin before Palm Sunday when Holy Week begins. The journey to the cross actually begins in the crib, but I have chosen to begin this 'real time' encounter on Mothering Sunday, the Fourth Sunday of Lent, with a reminder of those early days. The pace is slow at the beginning but it picks up as we get closer to the events we mark in the Triduum, the great 'Three Days' from Maundy Thursday evening until Easter Day. Then the pace slows again as we move through the Fifty Days to Pentecost.

For each stage in this journey there is a passage of scripture, a reflection and a prayer. For many of the stages there is a time suggested when you might read it; if you can, stick with the timings, so that you share the pace and feel the adrenalin rush of the events. This is in real time and should be in our real time.

Remember above everything that this all happened for you, Jesus entered our real time to enter your real time and bring you to eternity.

Lent 4

An early journey

Now every year his parents went to Jerusalem for the festival of the Passover. And when he was twelve years old, they went up as usual for the festival. When the festival was ended and they started to return, the boy Jesus stayed behind in Jerusalem, but his parents did not know it. Assuming that he was in the group of travellers, they went a day's journey. Then they started to look for him among their relatives and friends. When they did not find him, they returned to Jerusalem to search for him. After three days they found him in the temple, sitting among the teachers, listening to them and asking them questions. And all who heard him were amazed at his understanding and his answers. When his parents saw him they were astonished; and his mother said to him, 'Child, why have you treated us like this? Look, your father and I have been searching for you in great anxiety.' He said to them, 'Why were you searching for me? Did you not know that I must be in my Father's house?' But they did not understand what he said to them. Then he went down with them and came to Nazareth, and was obedient to them. His mother treasured all these things in her heart. And Jesus increased in wisdom and in years, and in divine and human favour. (Luke 2.41–52)

LENT 4

Journeys begin in so many different places. The journey to
Jerusalem for Jesus began very early on – when he was a
child it seems. It was a regular occurrence, so Luke tells us,
for Mary and Joseph to go up to Jerusalem for the Passover. But it was no day trip. Nazareth to Jerusalem was a
long journey and I suspect it could have been hazardous
– but they were travelling with a group of their relatives
and friends, which would have made it better and more
enjoyable. Perhaps they were all from the same synagogue
and this was what they did together.

Reading this passage again makes me realize just how
religious Jesus' upbringing was. This was a serious
commitment by his parents, to leave home and job and
community, every year for this religious festival at the very
heart of the nation and of their faith – Jerusalem and the
temple.

It also makes me realize that Jerusalem was not a strange
place to Jesus at all, it was all there in his background,
and I also wonder whether he continued to go up for the
festival every year, with his parents, relatives and friends
in those hidden years before his public ministry began.

Certainly it was a well-trodden path, therefore, from Galilee
to Jerusalem. Jesus knew the way like the back of his hand
and so when he finally set his face for Jerusalem and the
final journey he knew where he was going, in every sense.

Tracing the beginning of our journey might be a useful
thing to do as we approach Holy Week together. Who
have you travelled with? Where were you taken? Have
you walked well-trodden paths in your life – or do you
always search for new scenery?

I give thanks for my own journey to this point, this real point in time. I don't know precisely where I will be going next – none of us does – but I know that I can travel in confidence with the God who always travels with his people, through the familiar and the unfamiliar.

> God,
> some paths are familiar to me,
> I have travelled them many times before.
> Other paths are new
> and the terrain is unfamiliar.
> Wherever I go,
> give me the confidence that it is with you that I travel.
> Amen.

Passion Sunday

A dispute on the way

From that time on, Jesus began to show his disciples that he must go to Jerusalem and undergo great suffering at the hands of the elders and chief priests and scribes, and be killed, and on the third day be raised. And Peter took him aside and began to rebuke him, saying, 'God forbid it, Lord! This must never happen to you.' But he turned and said to Peter, 'Get behind me, Satan! You are a stumbling-block to me; for you are setting your mind not on divine things but on human things.'

Then Jesus told his disciples, 'If any want to become my followers, let them deny themselves and take up their cross and follow me. For those who want to save their life will lose it, and those who lose their life for my sake will find it. For what will it profit them if they gain the whole world but forfeit their life? Or what will they give in return for their life?

'For the Son of Man is to come with his angels in the glory of his Father, and then he will repay everyone for what has been done. Truly I tell you, there are some standing here who will not taste death before they see the Son of Man coming in his kingdom.' (Matthew 16.21–28)

What would they do? They had travelled with him for three years. They'd left everything they had, just dropped what they had – literally in some cases if you were anything like Peter with his fishing business – and followed him. And it had been fantastic – not easy – but fantastic. The things they had seen, the things that they had heard. Their life had taken such new turns. It was simply amazing and the effect on the people they met, the people who crowded round them and Jesus whenever they entered a town or a village, was amazing as well. They had seen the paralysed get up and walk; they had seen the blind recover their sight, the deaf their hearing and they had even seen the dead raised to life.

Deep down they knew that it couldn't go on like this for ever. After all, they were exhausted – they needed a break. It was all right for Jesus, not needing anywhere to lay his head, but they had left homes and family and everything, and a little bit of stability, well, it was attractive.

So when Jesus stuns them all by telling them that they are off to Jerusalem and that he will be killed there, well, is it any wonder that Peter reacted as he did? None of them knew what to say, really; none of them wanted to hear what Jesus was now saying. They weren't sure that they had signed up for this; it felt as though the rules of the game had suddenly changed.

> But ... as Peter had once said in a calmer moment, 'Lord, to whom can we go? You have the words of eternal life.' (John 6.68)

Not all invitations are welcome and not all tasks fill us with joy. It may be that it seems as though we have a choice but in fact there is no choice and we just have to accept where it is we have to go. Do we agree in a grudging way to the inevitable or accept the invitation with joy?

> Lord,
> I know there are things I have to do today
> that I would rather not do.
> May I do them
> filled with grace.
> Amen.

Saturday Before Palm Sunday

Take up your cross

While Jesus was going up to Jerusalem, he took the twelve disciples aside by themselves, and said to them on the way, 'See, we are going up to Jerusalem, and the Son of Man will be handed over to the chief priests and scribes, and they will condemn him to death; then they will hand him over to the Gentiles to be mocked and flogged and crucified; and on the third day he will be raised.'

Then the mother of the sons of Zebedee came to him with her sons, and kneeling before him, she asked a favour of him. And he said to her, 'What do you want?' She said to him, 'Declare that these two sons of mine will sit, one at your right hand and one at your left, in your kingdom.' But Jesus answered, 'You do not know what you are asking. Are you able to drink the cup that I am about to drink?' They said to him, 'We are able.' He said to them, 'You will indeed drink my cup, but to sit at my right hand and at my left, this is not mine to grant, but it is for those for whom it has been prepared by my Father.'

When the ten heard it, they were angry with the two brothers. But Jesus called them to him and said, 'You know that the rulers of the Gentiles lord it over them, and their great ones are tyrants over them. It will not be so among you; but whoever wishes to be great among you must be your servant, and whoever wishes to be first among you must be your slave; just as the Son of Man came not to be served but to serve, and to give his life a ransom for many.' (Matthew 20.17–28)

There must have been quite a crowd travelling with Jesus. There were the twelve but there was also, evidently, the mother of James and John and therefore one would imagine a number of other women as well, including Mary Magdalene and those who it says elsewhere 'ministered to him'. It must have been quite a sight, this group of 'out of towners' travelling along the road, maybe singing, certainly talking about what would happen when they arrived in the big city.

Jesus knew what was going to happen and he reminds the twelve again. They haven't forgotten what he said before. But now that Jerusalem is just a few hours' journey away they hear it with renewed force. But Jesus could be wrong of course. How did he know what was going to happen, what the chief priest and the scribes were planning? He might be entirely wrong, and after the feast of the Passover they could well be heading back along the road and back to their communities in Galilee. He might have got it all wrong.

The mother of James and John certainly had got it wrong and it was embarrassing to the others to watch her pleading for special favours for her boys. There was enough tension around without adding to it in this way.

8

In a few days' time as the cup is passed around the table by Jesus, this incident will come back to mind. They each drink from the cup and John will be there at Jesus' right hand at the table. And they will quickly discover that Jesus was right all along, that he knew exactly what he was doing and what the consequences would be. But now, in this brief pause on the journey, it is all still beyond their imagining.

There are times when we just don't get what's going on. For some reason there's tension in the room, in the office, and we don't know why. It's as though we missed out on something vital. Then it clicks into place and we catch up and understand. But those moments when we don't understand are unsettling.

> Lord,
> help me to listen well to others,
> to appreciate what others are saying
> and not to speak when I have nothing to say.
> Amen.

Palm Sunday

8.00am

A donkey for a king

When they had come near Jerusalem and had reached Bethphage, at the Mount of Olives, Jesus sent two disciples, saying to them, 'Go into the village ahead of you, and immediately you will find a donkey tied, and a colt with her; untie them and bring them to me. If anyone says anything to you, just say this, "The Lord needs them." And he will send them immediately.' This took place to fulfil what had been spoken through the prophet, saying,
  'Tell the daughter of Zion,
  Look, your king is coming to you,
  humble, and mounted on a donkey,
  and on a colt, the foal of a donkey.'
The disciples went and did as Jesus had directed them; they brought the donkey and the colt, and put their cloaks on them, and he sat on them. (Matthew 21.1–7)

The night had gone quickly. After the business on the road they made their way to a place where they could lodge. It was on the other side of the Mount of Olives. Those who had been before knew what a tremendous sight awaited them as they came across the mount and saw the city and the temple for the first time. It was a breathtaking sight.

They had walked a long way and after some food Jesus surprises them all by asking two of them to go off and get him a donkey. What was that all about? He never rode – he walked, they all walked! But he was insistent and seemed to know exactly where they would find one with its colt.

So they went and arrived back not much later with the donkey and the colt. Their cloaks went on to the donkey's back to make it easier to ride, and Jesus mounted and off they went.

As we reflect today, at this very moment pilgrims will be there now, on the Mount of Olives, waiting to walk the path that Jesus rode along. In churches around the world, palms and branches will have been gathered for the services today so that people can wave them and carry them. It's a triumphal beginning of the day and of the week. And of course that was the point of the donkey for Jesus, and Matthew quotes from the prophet Zechariah (Zechariah 9.9) in order that we get the reason. A humble king would ride on a donkey, a warrior would ride on a horse. Jesus is our humble king and this is his entry into the holy city where his crown and throne await him.

> Ride on, ride on, in majesty!
> In lowly pomp ride on to die!
> O Christ! Thy triumph now begins
> O'er captive death and conquered sin.
> (Henry Hart Milman, 1827)

9.00am

A cloud of witnesses

A very large crowd spread their cloaks on the road, and others cut branches from the trees and spread them on the road. The crowds that went ahead of him and that followed were shouting,
  'Hosanna to the Son of David!
  Blessed is the one who comes in the name of the Lord!
  Hosanna in the highest heaven!' (Matthew 21.8–9)

There's nothing like a procession to bring out the crowds and as Jesus, on the donkey, surrounded by his disciples, comes over the top of the Mount of Olives the excitement is palpable. The sight of the city never disappointed and everyone forgot the warnings that Jesus had given and got into party mood. Out from all the houses they passed people emerged and created a carpet of their cloaks and of the branches they pulled from the trees. It was amazing.

Egeria was a Galician woman who made a pilgrimage to the Holy Land in about 381–384. Like all good pilgrims she kept a journal of what she saw and experienced and it makes fascinating reading. This is what she wrote about Palm Sunday in Jerusalem.

And as the eleventh hour approaches, the passage from the Gospel is read, where the children, carrying branches and palms, met the Lord, saying; Blessed is He that cometh in the name of the Lord, and the bishop immediately rises, and all the people with him, and they all go on foot from the top of the Mount of Olives, all the people going before him with hymns and antiphons, answering one to another: Blessed is He that cometh in the Name of the Lord. And all the children in the neighbourhood, even those who are too young to walk, are carried by their parents on their shoulders, all of them bearing branches, some of palms and some of olives, and thus the bishop is escorted in the same manner as the Lord was of old. For all, even those of rank, both matrons and men, accompany the bishop all the way on foot in this manner, making these responses, from the top of the mount to the city, and thence through the whole city to the Anastasis, going very slowly lest the people should be wearied; and thus they arrive at the Anastasis at a late hour. And on arriving, although it is late, lucernare takes place, with prayer at the Cross; after which the people are dismissed.[1]

The Anastasis means, literally, the resurrection. So the crowd of worshippers headed straight for the church of the resurrection, of the Holy Sepulchre as we know it. It's just like our processions today. At Southwark Cathedral our annual procession begins in the Borough Market and ends in the church, in the place where resurrection is always celebrated.

So as we walk today we walk not only with Jesus but with past generations of Christians, 'a great cloud of witnesses' to use a wonderful phrase from the Letter to the Hebrews (Hebrews 12.1).

> True and humble king,
> hailed by the crowd as Messiah:
> grant us the faith to know you and love you,
> that we may be found beside you
> on the way of the cross,
> which is the path of glory.
> Amen.[2]

12.00 noon

Tears flow

> *As Jesus came near and saw the city, he wept over it,*
> *saying, 'If you, even you, had only recognized on this day*
> *the things that make for peace! But now they are hidden*
> *from your eyes. Indeed, the days will come upon you,*
> *when your enemies will set up ramparts around you and*
> *surround you, and hem you in on every side. They will*
> *crush you to the ground, you and your children within*
> *you, and they will not leave within you one stone upon*
> *another; because you did not recognize the time of your*
> *visitation from God.'* (Luke 19.41–44)

I find it reassuring to know that Jesus wept. This is not
the only place in the Gospels where Jesus cries. As he
approaches the tomb of his friend Lazarus he is overcome
with grief, and people see it and say: 'See how he loved
him' (John 11.36). It was out of love for his friend that he
wept and now out of love for the city, laid out before him,
that he weeps. The traditional site of where this happened
is on the slope of the Mount of Olives where there is a
beautiful, heart-stopping, tear-jerking view of the city

with the Dome of the Rock and the Golden Gate (bricked up of course) in front of you. The church that stands there, looked after by the Franciscans, is called 'Dominus Flevit' – 'The Lord wept' – and is shaped to look like a tear drop.

So what makes you cry? What makes me cry? In some ways I cry easily, to music or a film; but do I cry easily about what should make me weep – the injustice in the world, the plight of refugees, the homeless in our own city, child abuse, trafficking? The truth is I don't think I do. And I can't simply blame my Anglo-Saxon roots and a stiff-upper-lip mentality because it would be insincere to blame either of those things. I am in touch with my emotions, so why don't I weep for what I should weep for? Am I inured to it all in some way? But if it was good enough for Jesus, the right response for Jesus, then why not for me?

> Drop, drop, slow tears,
> And bathe those beauteous feet
> Which brought from Heaven
> The news and Prince of Peace:
> Cease not, wet eyes,
> His mercy to entreat;
> To cry for vengeance
> Sin doth never cease.
> In your deep floods
> Drown all my faults and fears;
> Nor let His eye
> See sin, but through my tears.
> (Phineas Fletcher, 1580–1650, 'A Litany')

5.00pm

The day ends

Then Jesus entered Jerusalem and went into the temple; and when he had looked around at everything, as it was already late, he went out to Bethany with the twelve. (Mark 11.11)

Matthew says that when Jesus entered into the city the place was in turmoil (Matthew 21.10), with people asking: 'Who is this?' Mark's account feels a great deal calmer, as though somehow the crowds and the commotion had died away after that triumphal entry and Jesus was able to wander around unnoticed. It had been a momentous day and though he was not left alone, Jesus knew that it wouldn't be long before the authorities reacted and he would be arrested. It was not as though he had arrived quietly, what with the donkey and the palms and the singing crowd accompanying him. But while people made comments as they approached the city, telling him to shut the crowds up, yet now everyone had disappeared and he was left with the twelve.

He had friends in Bethany and he knew that he could stay with them. It was the home of Mary, Martha and Lazarus. The hospitality and the conversation would be good and he would have the chance to relax, for a short while. Ironically, it meant retracing his steps, back to the Mount of Olives and over the other side to not far from where this morning began. But that was the only way of getting there. So gathering his friends he set off, back out of the city and to a place where he would be welcome.

And I hope each of us has somewhere where we feel relaxed and welcome. Our prayers are with those who do not.

> Keep watch, dear Lord,
> with those who wake, or watch, or weep this night,
> and give your angels charge over those who sleep.
> Tend the sick,
> give rest to the weary,
> sustain the dying,
> calm the suffering,
> and pity the distressed;
> all for your love's sake, O Christ our Redeemer.
> Amen.[3]

Monday in Holy Week

9.00am

Figs

> *On the following day, when they came from Bethany, Jesus was hungry. Seeing in the distance a fig tree in leaf, he went to see whether perhaps he would find anything on it. When he came to it, he found nothing but leaves, for it was not the season for figs. He said to it, 'May no one ever eat fruit from you again.' And his disciples heard it.* (Mark 11.12–14)

Not everything is quite how we would like it. I'm not sure about these verses from St Mark's Gospel – what do I make of them? If it wasn't the season for figs then no wonder that Jesus didn't find any on the tree. So why react so angrily? Is this really how Jesus would behave?

The writer of the Letter to the Hebrews is quite clear that Jesus did not sin.

We do not have a high priest who is unable to sympathize with our weaknesses, but we have one who in every respect has been tested as we are, yet without sin. Let us therefore approach the throne of grace with boldness, so that we may receive mercy and find grace to help in time of need. (Hebrews 4.15–16)

In one sense, of course, it is encouraging that Jesus might have sympathy with me when I come out with a petulant and inappropriate reaction to something. But that is not what this passage is about.

It would seem that rather than talking about figs Jesus was talking about other fruit, the fruit that was not being produced by the people of God. So just as he would go on to talk about the destruction of the temple in these days in the lead up to his Passion, so he is talking here about the way in which the unfruitfulness of the people would be overthrown and a new fruitfulness in a new kingdom established – and established in him.

So perhaps we need to begin today by thinking about the extent to which our own life is fruitful. Are we the producers of good fruit? St Paul lists what the fruit of those who are alive in the spirit might be:

The fruit of the Spirit is love, joy, peace, patience, kindness, generosity, faithfulness, gentleness, and self-control. (Galatians 5.22–23)

It could be the basis for an audit of our life. Where am I being fruitful, where in my life is fruit not being produced?

For Jesus this new day was just beginning and he was making his way back into the city to face whatever was waiting for him there. For us this day is beginning as well. Some of us will already be at work, some enjoying a break from school or tasks, some at the kinds of activities that take up our time and attention every day. But whatever it is we are doing, let us hope it is a day of fruitfulness.

> Lord, I shall be very busy this day.
> If I forget thee, do not thou forget me.
> (Sir Jacob Astley at the Battle of Edgehill, 1642)

11.00am

Turning the tables

They came to Jerusalem. And Jesus entered the temple and began to drive out those who were selling and those who were buying in the temple, and he overturned the tables of the money-changers and the seats of those who sold doves; and he would not allow anyone to carry anything through the temple. He was teaching and saying, 'Is it not written,

"My house shall be called a house of prayer for all the nations"?

But you have made it a den of robbers.'

And when the chief priests and the scribes heard it, they kept looking for a way to kill him; for they were afraid of him, because the whole crowd was spellbound by his teaching. (Mark 11.15–18)

It was a day for the big statements, at the fig tree and now in the temple, at the very heart of the establishment. It is impossible for us to imagine a similar context, though St Peter's Basilica in Rome comes close to it. But there was only one temple and therefore it was the focus of the religious and national attention in a way that Westminster Abbey for us isn't quite.

It was the week of the festival and the place was busier than usual, a perfect time to make this kind of grand gesture, this statement of intent, the throwing down of the gauntlet, the acting out of the manifesto for change that Jesus had brought with him into the city.

The temple complex was made up of a series of courts – the outer one where Gentiles were permitted and then successive ones which were progressively for more and more important people, women, men, the priests, the high priest. At the very heart of the place was the Holy of Holies, which only the high priest could enter and then only once a year. It was a physical representation of a particular view of heaven in which only the chosen could get close to God.

It was in the outer courts that the selling would be done and the money-changing and the business. Holy places tend to attract that kind of thing, but here it was not simply the first-century equivalent of the selling of postcards but selling access to God and fleecing those who wished to make their offering.

St John says that Jesus made a whip of cords (John 2.15) and drove out the sellers and the money-changers, overturning their tables, scattering the animals, and in justification screaming out a passage from the prophet Isaiah (Isaiah 56.7). That passage gives the game away. Jesus wanted to overturn the whole system that kept people away from God – 'a house of prayer for all nations'. Jesus says in St John's Gospel:

'And I, when I am lifted up from the earth, will draw all people to myself.' (John 12.32)

The whip of cords would soon be turned on Jesus and he would be made a sacrificial offering rather than one of these animals. But as it all happens, the veil of the temple will be torn in two and all will be overthrown as the earth itself quakes. The cleansing of the temple was just a first, violent step in a violent but revolutionary week.

But are we still keeping people away from God; is our church as inclusive as Christ desires it to be?

> Loving God,
> your arms extend to including even me.
> May your church be a home for all people
> and may none be turned away.
> Amen.

6.oopm

The tidal flow

When evening came, Jesus and his disciples went out of the city. (Mark 11.19)

In these first days of Holy Week Jesus was making his way backwards and forwards, in and out of the city, lodging, most probably, in Bethany with his friends. The path he was taking went from the city and across the Kidron valley, then up the Mount of Olives past the Garden of Gethsemane and down the other side. This is familiar territory for us all in Holy Week, places where dramatic things would take place.

Now though it is just the way to a place of rest. It has been a dramatic day.

Crowds of people, day in, day out, surge across London Bridge, past Southwark Cathedral, going to and from the City and their desks. T. S. Eliot records this human 'flow' in his epic poem 'The Waste Land'. The flow on the bridge mirrors the flow of the river beneath.

Wordsworth, in his poem 'Composed upon Westminster Bridge, September 3, 1802', picks up something of that calm, gliding, backwards and forwards tidal flow.

Ne'er saw I, never felt, a calm so deep!
The river glideth at his own sweet will:
Dear God! the very houses seem asleep;
And all that mighty heart is lying still!

And each of us, like Jesus, looks for that calm, for the rest we need to face the ebb and flow of the following day.

Lighten our darkness,
we beseech thee, O Lord;
and by thy great mercy
defend us from all perils
and dangers of this night;
for the love of thy only Son,
our Saviour, Jesus Christ.
Amen.[4]

Tuesday in Holy Week

9.00am

Have faith

In the morning as they passed by, they saw the fig tree withered away to its roots. Then Peter remembered and said to Jesus, 'Rabbi, look! The fig tree that you cursed has withered.' Jesus answered them, 'Have faith in God. Truly I tell you, if you say to this mountain, "Be taken up and thrown into the sea", and if you do not doubt in your heart, but believe that what you say will come to pass, it will be done for you. So I tell you, whatever you ask for in prayer, believe that you have received it, and it will be yours.' (Mark 11.20–24)

The cursing of the fig tree the morning before had caused the tree to wither, and the disciples notice this as, after a night of sleep, they make their way back into the city. This time Jesus uses the tree as an opportunity to talk about prayer.

So often in the Gospels we are told that, where there is no doubt, faith is effective. In St Matthew's Gospel Jesus speaks of faith, 'the size of a mustard seed' (Matthew 17.20), being able to move mountains. I find this challenging. I pray every day and not just at the set times for prayer with my colleagues in the cathedral. But how big is my faith? Is there doubt lurking deep within? I suspect, to be honest, that there is and the beginning of this day of Holy Week challenges me personally.

I have never learnt to swim – all the school lessons I received just didn't achieve it. What holds me back is a fear that I cannot conquer. People say to me: 'Just let yourself go; trust in the water; you won't sink.' But, so far, I haven't believed them. So I can't swim. This is the closest experience that I have that I think reflects upon prayer. We have to have the faith, the courage to throw ourselves completely upon God, upon God's love and mercy and not hold on to the doubt, the disbelief that is not about healthy questioning but unhealthy denying. Jesus asks us not to hold ourselves back but to swim freely in God's love, to swim freely in prayer.

> Lord, in every need let me come to you
> with humble trust saying,
> 'Jesus, help me.'
>
> In all my doubts, perplexities,
> and temptations,
> Jesus, help me.
>
> In hours of loneliness,
> weariness, and trials,
> Jesus, help me.

In the failure of my plans and hopes;
in disappointments, troubles, and sorrows,
Jesus, help me.

When others fail me
and your grace alone can assist me,
Jesus, help me.

When I throw myself on your tender love,
as a father and saviour,
Jesus, help me.

When my heart is cast down by failure
at seeing no good come from my efforts,
Jesus, help me.

When I feel impatient
and my cross irritates me,
Jesus, help me.

When I am ill and my head and hands cannot work
and I am lonely,
Jesus, help me.

Always, always, in spite of weakness,
falls, and shortcomings of every kind,
Jesus, help me and never forsake me.
Amen.[5]

11.00am

By what authority?

When Jesus entered the temple, the chief priests and the elders of the people came to him as he was teaching, and said, 'By what authority are you doing these things, and who gave you this authority?' Jesus said to them, 'I will also ask you one question; if you tell me the answer, then I will also tell you by what authority I do these things. Did the baptism of John come from heaven, or was it of human origin?' And they argued with one another, 'If we say, "From heaven", he will say to us, "Why then did you not believe him?" But if we say, "Of human origin", we are afraid of the crowd; for all regard John as a prophet.' So they answered Jesus, 'We do not know.' And he said to them, 'Neither will I tell you by what authority I am doing these things.' (Matthew 21.23–27)

So Jesus comes back to the scene of his outburst of anger on the previous day. The chief priests and the elders are waiting for him. They must have known that he would be back, that that was not his final word, not his final action. But they weren't ready to arrest him, not just yet.

So instead they ask him a question – about his authority, by what, by whose authority was he doing these things.

They felt challenged. He was only one man from out of town, not part of the hierarchy in any way, but he had disciples, fervent disciples and when he spoke people flocked to hear him. In response to their question Jesus then raises the name of someone else who challenged religious and national leaders, John the Baptist. John had gone through his own passion, his arrest, his imprisonment and then his martyrdom at the hands of Herod. That was still fresh in everyone's memory, it had caused huge distress among Jesus' own disciples, many who had begun to follow him after they left following John (John 1.37).

The chief priests spotted the trap that Jesus had set for them. Whatever they answered about John would catch them out, and so they back off and say: 'We do not know.'

In St Matthew's Gospel Jesus tells his disciples that they are to be 'as wise as serpents and innocent as doves' (Matthew 10.16). It was good advice and we still need to listen to it and understand its implications. The church, Christians, are not apart from the world, they are part of the world. While we don't want to operate as the world so often operates, at the same time we can't allow ourselves to be out manoeuvred by those who are more wily and swift-footed than we are. Spending as much time as I do in the City of London and in a whole variety of meetings, I have to remind myself of the serpent and the dove. By inclination I am a dove but I can't ignore the call to have something of the serpent in me as well.

In Jesus we see both – wisdom and innocence – the serpent and the dove. And as, in a few days, we will see him standing before Pilate and before Herod, who had John beheaded, we will see his determination at work again but with subtlety and with power.

The famous prayer of St Francis of Assisi calls on us to be peacemakers but we can only do this as Francis worked for the rebuilding of the church, with grit and determination.

> Lord, make me an instrument of your peace;
> Where there is hatred, let me sow love;
> Where there is injury, pardon;
> Where there is error, truth;
> Where there is doubt, faith;
> Where there is despair, hope;
> Where there is darkness, light;
> And where there is sadness, joy.
> O Divine Master,
> Grant that I may not so much seek
> To be consoled as to console;
> To be understood as to understand;
> To be loved as to love.
> For it is in giving that we receive;
> It is in pardoning that we are pardoned;
> And it is in dying that we are born to eternal life.
> Amen.

1.00pm

We want to see Jesus

Now among those who went up to worship at the festival were some Greeks. They came to Philip, who was from Bethsaida in Galilee, and said to him, 'Sir, we wish to see Jesus.' Philip went and told Andrew; then Andrew and Philip went and told Jesus. Jesus answered them, 'The hour has come for the Son of Man to be glorified. Very truly, I tell you, unless a grain of wheat falls into the earth and dies, it remains just a single grain; but if it dies, it bears much fruit. Those who love their life lose it, and those who hate their life in this world will keep it for eternal life. Whoever serves me must follow me, and where I am, there will my servant be also. Whoever serves me, the Father will honour.' (John 12.20–26)

They too were from out of town, and not just from out of town but from another place and another culture. These unnamed Greeks approached Philip for a meeting with Jesus, for a way into the inner circle. Philip had a Greek name and we can perhaps infer from this that he spoke Greek. The tradition is that he later went on to preach and

33

witness to the gospel in Greece and other Greek-speaking places. So these men – we don't know that they are men but they most probably were – find a kindred spirit, someone who understands them, in order to find out more.

In St Matthew's Gospel Jesus makes it quite clear that he has been called to minister to the 'lost sheep of the House of Israel' (Matthew 15.24) and in his dealings with the Syro-Phoenician woman is less than complimentary in the language he uses: 'It is not right to take the children's bread and throw it to the dogs' (Matthew 15.26). But in fact, despite these instances when Jesus appears to have a very clear and particular focus for his mission, there is an inclusiveness in the way he sees the kingdom – that it has open borders.

There are no niceties in the account of the meeting, however. Instead Jesus comes out with this powerful image:

> *'Unless a grain of wheat falls into the earth and dies, it remains just a single grain; but if it dies, it bears much fruit.'* (John 12:24)

There has to be death for life to flourish is what Jesus is saying to them and to us. It is an image that has helped us to understand his Passion but also to bring understanding to all the martyrdoms that have occurred in the history of the church up to and including today. Many seeds have fallen into the soil and produced a rich harvest, as in the parable of the sower (Matthew 13.1–9). Philip was listening to this along with the Greeks whom he had brought to Jesus, and perhaps he might not have understood the relevance of those words to him then – but later he would do.

Each of us is called to mission and witness, and people may ask us about Jesus because we appear to be a kindred sprit, share their language, share their outlook, share something of their background – like the Greeks and Philip. All we can do is respond and allow ourselves to be the wheat grain that bears fruit for an open-bordered kingdom.

> God, may I bear kingdom fruit
> In the rich soil of your love.
> Amen.

4.00pm

Spying out Jesus

So they watched him and sent spies who pretended to be honest, in order to trap him by what he said, so as to hand him over to the jurisdiction and authority of the governor. (Luke 20.20)

They were on to him; he was being watched; his group was being infiltrated. It isn't just we who have invented a spy and surveillance culture, its not just the invention of John le Carré and his ilk, the stuff of James Bond and *Spooks*. The decision had been made that he had to be arrested, that for the sake of the nation, for their own sakes, this troublemaker had to be stopped. But they weren't an uncivilized mob – yet – they needed evidence, they had laws and it was important that they kept to the law. So they sent in the spies, pretending to be honest, pretending to be sincere, but listening for the word with which they could bring him down.

It's the serpent and dove business again. Jesus must have been aware that this was going on, he must have known what tricks they were playing. But he doesn't stop doing what he has to do. In St John's Gospel Jesus says:

'My father is still working and I also am working.' (John 5.17)

The Gospels, not least St Matthew's Gospel, are full of the teaching that Jesus was giving in these days – parables, warnings. His words were clear and they were strong. He wasn't pulling his punches at all, even though there were those in the crowd listening to him who were noting what he said and would be only too willing to repeat his words and twist his words as required.

You can't live looking over your shoulder – that's the way to a form of paranoia. Should I only say from the pulpit what people want to hear or things that won't rock the boat? It is something I often think about. I have burnt my fingers before, and by saying things which others have objected to I have damaged the ministry of the cathedral and of others in the diocese. And it isn't just good enough to say, 'Well, that is what I believe in', or to use God as the excuse: 'It was God who told me to say this.' But we have to speak truth to power, that is the calling of the church and the prophetic ministry in which all Christians share. And it is not just the power 'out there' to which we speak truth; the church also needs to hear truth and that is often spoken from beyond the high walls of the ecclesiastical culture. Our enemies will be listening to catch us out, but if we don't speak the truth how are we being faithful to our calling?

Reinhold Neibuhr is, by repute, former President Obama's favourite theologian. His 'Prayer of Serenity' is one we might offer in the face of the dilemmas that sometimes beset us.

> God, grant me the serenity
> to accept the things I cannot change,
> the courage to change the things I can
> and the wisdom to know the difference.

6.00pm

All will be thrown down

> *As Jesus came out of the temple and was going away, his disciples came to point out to him the buildings of the temple. Then he asked them, 'You see all these, do you not? Truly I tell you, not one stone will be left here upon another; all will be thrown down.'* (Matthew 24.1–2)

I said that people were listening for what Jesus said to catch him out. Jesus is leaving the city once again. We have seen him doing this each day since his triumphant arrival on Palm Sunday. At the west end of the temple was a magnificent flight of steps; the pilgrims would have entered and exited the temple using these steps. Pilgrims to the Holy Land today can see them and walk on them. They are a magnificent flight and even with the passage of the years they are still impressive. You can easily imagine the disciples with Jesus, coming out of the outer court and heading down the steps and being overawed with the scale of the place. All the evidence suggests that this was one of the wonders of the world, simply magnificent and in its magnificence something of a glimpse of heaven.

And as they are standing there, taking it all in, Jesus says that the whole thing will be destroyed. Each of the Synoptic Gospels (Matthew, Mark and Luke) contain shorter or longer accounts of this teaching. It is like the fig tree, Jesus is actually talking about the temple of his body and the resurrection. But it is also true that the temple was destroyed in AD 70 and was never reconstructed.

But his words would be repeated back to him by the spies when he comes to trial.

> May the words of my mouth and the meditation of
>   my heart
> be pleasing to you,
> O Lord, my rock and my redeemer.
> (Psalm 19.14)

10.00pm

Time out

Every day Jesus was teaching in the temple, and at night he would go out and spend the night on the Mount of Olives, as it was called. And all the people would get up early in the morning to listen to him in the temple. (Luke 21.37–38)

Another day ends. Luke suggests that rather than heading over the Mount of Olives into Bethany Jesus stayed on the Mount itself. We know from other references in the gospels that Jesus was in the habit of taking himself off, finding space to be alone and to pray. There are occasions in Galilee when he tries to get time on his own and then people follow him because they have discovered where he has taken himself to and want to be with him. Was this evening one of those occasions, when he just needed to get away from everyone else, even his closest friends, and clear his head and say his prayers?

It can be difficult to find time alone and especially when we share our life with others. Is it right to go into a room and sit on my own when the family are all together, when I should be attending to their needs? It may be that we feel selfish if we think that 'I' have needs that need to be met, that 'I' can give time to myself.

But the truth is that however much we may be devoted to family and friends, we can't keep on giving without receiving and we can't receive unless we are open to that and available to that. The biggest temptation that I struggle with, and fail at miserably, is an inability to say 'no' and a reluctance not to be active but to simply sit and 'be'. But, as I am often reminded by those who care for me, you can't continue to help others unless you help yourself as well.

Those of us who have flown will be familiar with the safety demonstration that the air stewards perform before take-off. We are shown the safety card and the brace position, the inflatable jacket and the oxygen mask. When the latter is presented to us we're told, 'first put on your own mask before helping someone else', or words to that effect. It is counter-cultural. I must help my neighbour first and then myself. But you can't, certainly not in that situation. You will be of no use dead!

Look on prayer and rest and reflection as the oxygen for the soul that you need. Look at time on your own as the oxygen mask that you need in order to be the servant of others. Jesus took himself off to be alone; so why wouldn't we?

> Lord, may I rest in you tonight
> and wake refreshed,
> ready to serve you
> and my neighbour tomorrow.
> Amen.

Wednesday in Holy Week

9.00am

A reality check

Jesus said to his disciples, 'You know that after two days the Passover is coming, and the Son of Man will be handed over to be crucified.' (Matthew 26.1–2)

It was a wake-up call, almost literally. This was the fourth day that they had been in Jerusalem. So far, each day had followed a similar pattern – entering the city, Jesus teaching, confronting, challenging the leadership of the temple and the Jewish people, the crowds listening to his teaching and then Jesus leaving the city as darkness fell. Now he warns them again what will happen. It's only two days to the feast of the Passover and tensions are rising. The city is full of Roman soldiers ready to put down any sign of trouble. Jesus is no 'trouble-maker' but he could easily be seen to be one by those who would like to be rid of him, and there were plenty of those about. So Jesus' words to them were something of a reality check as once more they began the journey into the city and whatever awaited them today.

The day may have a familiar routine to us but we can easily be surprised by the unexpected happening, the thing we had never planned for, blowing us off course, upsetting the apple cart of our day. And however well prepared we may be, there is always that that will turn round and bite us when we least expect it. Yet, there is no option but to enter the city, to make the familiar journey into an unfamiliar day and to keep faith that in the expected and the unexpected God is with us.

The prayer of Dag Hammarskjöld is perhaps the easiest to read and the hardest to pray. Hammarskjöld was a Swedish diplomat, economist and author. The second and the youngest Secretary General of the United Nations, he served from April 1953 until his death in a plane crash in September 1961. He is one of just three people to be awarded a posthumous Nobel Prize. The prayer from his book *Markings* is the one below. Pray it if you have the courage to mean it today!

> **For all that has been – thanks.**
> **For all that will be – yes.**

11.00am

Holding nothing back

Jesus sat down opposite the treasury, and watched the crowd putting money into the treasury. Many rich people put in large sums. A poor widow came and put in two small copper coins, which are worth a penny. Then he called his disciples and said to them, 'Truly I tell you, this poor widow has put in more than all those who are contributing to the treasury. For all of them have contributed out of their abundance; but she out of her poverty has put in everything she had, all she had to live on.' (Mark 12.41–44)

The Women's Court was where the thirteen collecting boxes were located which fed the treasury. They were shaped like trumpets and maybe this is what Jesus was referring to in Matthew 6.2 when he talks about trumpeting almsgiving! The boxes were designated for different kinds of giving. One was for money that would have paid for the offering of a turtledove; one was for the wood for the sacrifices; others were for the golden vessels; others for the temple tribute, the half shekel, that had to be paid.

It was here that Jesus settled down after entering the temple. He was doing what I really enjoy doing, watching people. It can be fascinating, just watching what others do. And among the many people milling around and putting their money into the 'trumpets', he sees an old woman. He knew she was a widow from the way that she was dressed, and watching her intently he saw what she gave, two coins, a penny. It was not a great deal but it was, for her, everything that she had.

'Commit your way to the LORD; trust in him, and he will act' (Psalm 37.5). It's easier said than done, to give away all you have and to trust in the Lord. But it looks like this is what the poor widow did. It was everything that she had to give; she held nothing back, she committed herself to the Lord. Jesus is so moved by what he sees that he calls the twelve to him and points out what the woman has done.

Soon Jesus will be asked to give everything, his life, his self, and to hold nothing back. He is fully committed to God; a challenge to my own lack of commitment.

> Generous God,
> in Jesus you have given yourself to me;
> may I give myself to you
> and hold nothing back.
> Amen.

12.00 noon

Who are you?

> *Then the chief priests and the elders of the people gathered in the palace of the high priest, who was called Caiaphas, and they conspired to arrest Jesus by stealth and kill him. But they said, 'Not during the festival, or there may be a riot among the people.'* (Matthew 26.3–5)

The names begin to appear, the characters in the drama are now evolving before our eyes. So far the people named have been Jesus and some of the disciples. But now other names begin to appear in the gospel narratives, real people who land us in real time, in real history – people like Caiaphas.

According to the first-century historian Josephus, this person was Joseph ben Caiaphas who was high priest from AD 18 to 36. He was a real person with real responsibilities and he and his five brothers led the Jewish community between the years AD 6 and 63. Other names will be added to his – Pilate, Joseph of Arimathea. We know that

Nicodemus was there and Gamaliel, sympathetic Jewish leaders who were interested in what Jesus had to say.

It is easy to imagine that the gospel is timeless because in one sense it is, always relevant, always new. But from the beginning of the accounts of the Evangelists they are keen to fix it in history. Luke gives us a set of historical coordinates in his Gospel

> *In the fifteenth year of the reign of Emperor Tiberius, when Pontius Pilate was governor of Judea, and Herod was ruler of Galilee, and his brother Philip ruler of the region of Ituraea and Trachonitis, and Lysanias ruler of Abilene, during the high-priesthood of Annas and Caiaphas, the word of God came to John son of Zechariah in the wilderness.* (Luke 3.1–2)

This is not God entering human experience out of time, out of history, but in time, in history, in real time, in real circumstances, with real people whose names we know and of whom evidence can be found. This is a powerful reminder to those who dismiss our faith as fantasy. Jesus is historical and the events of the crucifixion are historical. Of course, faith comes into play in how we interpret the history, but of the history I have no doubt.

And we are creatures of history, born in time, living in real time. I have had fun tracing my ancestors; I have got back to the beginning of the eighteenth century when my maternal family line were farm labourers in the Midlands and my paternal line were cabinet makers in Ipswich. They are like guy ropes fixing the tent of my being into real history. The TV programme *Who Do You Think You Are?* allows us to see 'celebrities' discovering themselves.

48

Holy Week encourages us to discover our real self along-side Jesus, who roots us in real time.

> Everlasting God,
> in whom we live and move and have our being:
> you have made us for yourself,
> and hearts are restless until they rest in you. Amen.
> (St Augustine of Hippo)

3.00pm

The ends don't justify the means

*It was two days before the Passover and the festival
of Unleavened Bread. The chief priests and the scribes
were looking for a way to arrest Jesus by stealth and kill
him; for they said, 'Not during the festival, or there may
be a riot among the people.'* (Mark 14.1–2)

They would go to any lengths – stealth, murder – to secure
what they wanted to happen, to get Jesus out of the way,
out of their hair, once and for all. So many people think
that the ends justify the means but this just isn't true.
You may have the very best intentions as a motive, but
if the means are immoral, will the ends provide justification? Hiroshima, Iraq, Libya, actions that appear to have
surrounded the investigation into the death of Stephen
Lawrence, the fire at Grenfell Tower – life on a large
scale and on a small is littered with the results of immoral
actions that could never deliver the good intentions that
led to them.

But I shouldn't point the finger at anyone else when, if I examine my own ambitions, my own actions, my own intentions, they are mixed to say the least and I wouldn't want them all examined in public.

Jesus is slowly becoming the victim of huge injustice as this week progresses.

> Almighty and most merciful Father,
> we have wandered and strayed from your ways
> like lost sheep.
> We have followed too much the devices and desires
> of our own hearts.
> We have offended against your holy laws.
> We have left undone those things
> that we ought to have done;
> and we have done those things
> that we ought not to have done;
> and there is no health in us.
> But you, O Lord, have mercy upon us sinners.
> Spare those who confess their faults.
> Restore those who are penitent,
> according to your promises declared to mankind
> in Christ Jesus our Lord.
> And grant, O most merciful Father, for his sake,
> that we may live a disciplined, righteous and godly life,
> to the glory of your holy name.
> Amen.[6]

6.oopm

At the margins

*Now while Jesus was at Bethany in the house of Simon
the leper, a woman came to him with an alabaster jar of
very costly ointment, and she poured it on his head as
he sat at the table. But when the disciples saw it, they
were angry and said, 'Why this waste? For this ointment
could have been sold for a large sum, and the money
given to the poor.' But Jesus, aware of this, said to them,
'Why do you trouble the woman? She has performed a
good service for me. For you always have the poor with
you, but you will not always have me. By pouring this
ointment on my body she has prepared me for burial.
Truly I tell you, wherever this good news is proclaimed
in the whole world, what she has done will be told in
remembrance of her.' (Matthew 26.6–13)*

Jesus was back in Bethany, now in Simon's house where
this dramatic and beautiful event takes place. After his
death, the women would bring oil to anoint his body for
burial and this unnamed woman pre-empts that final act
of love by anointing him now. In the Coronation Rite

in this country the anointing oil, which contains oils of orange, roses, cinnamon, musk and ambergris, is poured from the Ampulla into the Anointing Spoon and then on to the head of the monarch. The Ampulla is believed to be the one first used in the coronation of Henry IV in 1399 and the golden spoon is certainly of the thirteenth century. It is the very ancient way of anointing and goes back to Old Testament times.

So Jesus is anointed not just for burial but as a king – the King of the Jews, as he would be proclaimed from the cross, Jesus Christ, Universal King as we know him.

But as I read this passage something else stuck out at me. He was in the 'house of Simon the leper'. Was this a person whom he had healed, a former leper he had touched and made clean? Lepers were complete outsiders, they lived outside the camp in the Old Testament, they lived outside the village or the city in Jesus' day. They were the excluded of society. But Jesus is the one who suffers 'outside the camp' as it says in the Letter to the Hebrews

> *Jesus also suffered outside the city gate in order to sanc-*
> *tify the people by his own blood. Let us then go to him*
> *outside the camp and bear the abuse he endured.*
> (Hebrews 13.12–13)

He identifies himself with the marginalized, with the excluded, and our redemption is won beyond the walls, where those shut off from society were. Simon knew this and that must be why he invited Jesus for dinner. Others still labelled him for who he was, 'the leper', but Jesus loves him for who he truly is, Simon, brought back by the one who reached out and touched untouchables.

Who are beyond our walls – did Jesus, king, saviour, friend bring you in from the cold?

> Jesus,
> your love embraces all,
> your arms stretched wide on the cross
> encompass all.
> May I love as you love,
> for you love even me.
> Amen.

10.00pm

Spy Wednesday

Then one of the twelve, who was called Judas Iscariot, went to the chief priests and said, 'What will you give me if I betray him to you?' They paid him thirty pieces of silver. And from that moment he began to look for an opportunity to betray him. (Matthew 26.14–16)

The traditional name for this day that is now almost over is 'Spy Wednesday'. The name comes from these verses, which record that the chief priests got what they wanted, someone on the inside who would hand Jesus to them on a plate. Just to sweeten the pill he got an up-front payment. They trusted him, they trusted him (can you believe it?), trusted this one who was prepared to betray the Rabbi he had been following for three years – to be the spy they needed. Judas presents himself as the one with a social conscience when he objects to the anointing of Jesus on the basis that the money could be given to the poor. The Gospel puts a gloss on this:

He said this not because he cared about the poor, but because he was a thief; he kept the common purse and used to steal what was put into it. (John 12.6)

But maybe he did share in God's option for the poor; maybe he was misguided; maybe, as some commentators and Andrew Lloyd Webber and Tim Rice in *Jesus Christ Superstar* suggest, he was trying to provoke the situation to get Jesus to act in the way he thought he should. After all, his name – Iscariot – may refer to a kind of knife; it could suggest that he could be a bit of a troublemaker.

But whatever the truth, the trusted man breaks the trust, takes the money and agrees to the deed. And he does it in the dark so that his misdeeds cannot be seen. As it says in John's Gospel

For all who do evil hate the light and do not come to the light, so that their deeds may not be exposed. (John 3.20)

But Jesus is the light of world and we are called to walk and act in the light. This ancient song has been sung by the church as the vesper light is lit. This translation of 'Phos Hilaron' is by Robert Bridges (1844–1930).

O gladsome light, O grace
Of God the Father's face,
The eternal splendour wearing;
Celestial, holy, blest,
Our Saviour Jesus Christ,
Joyful in thine appearing.

Now, ere day fadeth quite,
We see the evening light,
Our wonted hymn outpouring;
Father of might unknown,
Thee, his incarnate Son,
And Holy Spirit adoring.

To thee of right belongs
All praise of holy songs,
O Son of God, Lifegiver;
Thee, therefore, O Most High,
The world doth glorify,
And shall exalt forever.

Maundy Thursday

9.00am

Shattering the norms

On the first day of Unleavened Bread the disciples came to Jesus, saying, 'Where do you want us to make the preparations for you to eat the Passover?' He said, 'Go into the city to a certain man, and say to him, "The Teacher says, My time is near; I will keep the Passover at your house with my disciples."' (Matthew 26.17–18)

It was a big day, and not just for Jesus and the disciples. People were making their preparations for the festival and for the meal that was an integral part – *the* integral part – of what would happen. So the disciples are keen, as soon as it is morning, to get the arrangements in place. They are still outside the city; perhaps this takes place in Bethany. After all, Jesus says to them, 'Go into the city.' It was there, at the very heart of the nation, at the very heart of the faith, that Jesus wanted them to gather.

Luke provides a little more information than Matthew to help the disciples with their task:

> *'Listen,' Jesus said to them, 'when you have entered the city, a man carrying a jar of water will meet you; follow him into the house he enters and say to the owner of the house, "The teacher asks you, 'Where is the guest room, where I may eat the Passover with my disciples?'"" He will show you a large room upstairs, already furnished. Make preparations for us there.'* (Luke 22.10–12)

There is something strange about all this. This person would be obvious. It was a MAN carrying a water jar. This was woman's work not man's work. No self-respecting man would be seen doing something like this, carrying a jar of water. Jesus, as a boy, would have been to the well in Nazareth with his mother Mary; he had talked to the woman at the well in Samaria, but it remained the work women did.

Isn't it typical that the man whose house Jesus wanted to eat this pivotal, universe-changing meal in, would be someone who was so humble that he would risk scorn in doing this work, so counter-cultural that he could step outside the norms, was a modern man in an ancient world.

Being a priest, being a bishop has for too long been seen to be man's work. Now we know it is the work of the people of God – men and women, gay and straight, black and white. The man who led the disciples to the room all prepared for them was prepared to shatter social norms and he was a friend of Jesus. What does Jesus make of a church that so often bolsters stereotypes and injustice?

Lord, break us free
from old ways of thinking
from old ways of living;
liberate us
to live like you
to think like you
to be your body
in the world.
Amen.

12.00 noon

The waiting begins

So the disciples did as Jesus had directed them, and they prepared the Passover meal. (Matthew 26.19)

When they got into the city, they found the man, followed him and entered the room, where all was ready. It was quiet; just the noise of what was going on outside in the street as people made their way backwards and forwards, caught up in their own preparations.

Now all they could do was wait for Jesus to arrive ...

In the midst of a busy world,
we wait, Lord,
with you
and for you.
Amen.

5.00pm

The evening begins

When it was evening, he took his place with the twelve; and while they were eating, he said, 'Truly I tell you, one of you will betray me.' And they became greatly distressed and began to say to him one after another, 'Surely not I, Lord?' He answered, 'The one who has dipped his hand into the bowl with me will betray me. The Son of Man goes as it is written of him, but woe to that one by whom the Son of Man is betrayed! It would have been better for that one not to have been born.' Judas, who betrayed him, said, 'Surely not I, Rabbi?' He replied, 'You have said so.' (Matthew 26.20–25)

Eventually the waiting was over and Jesus and the other disciples arrived. They came in and settled down. It is a most familiar scene for us. The fresco of the Last Supper by Leonardo da Vinci has given us an image of the meal in the Upper Room that is almost impossible to remove from our heads. Of course, it is painted as a director of a programme on TV would have to film it. Da Vinci has everyone seated unnaturally, on one side of the table. All we are told in the Gospel is that 'Jesus took his place'. He, though, as 'the head of the household', would have taken the place reserved for the head, for the host of this meal, and the others would be gathered round him.

One of the many changes that occurred in the last century to the way in which we celebrate the Eucharist was that the president moved to the other side of the altar. Instead of only seeing the back of the priest, the priest now faced us across the table and we faced the priest. It is a much more natural, human way of presiding. In Southwark Cathedral, because of the altars that we have, some of the Eucharists are 'back to the people' and others in this 'face to face' mode. Each has value of course, but as one who presides the experience is so different when you are, as it were, gathering the people of God around the altar as opposed to standing with them behind you.

For the Eucharist is the supreme act of encounter with God and with one another as family, as community, because a meal always is. Learning to value the Eucharist as the family meal, as much as anything else, is something that we have to work at. It is the most sublime spiritual experience but it is also the experience of simply sharing food and drink, and as they gather at the table with Jesus that is what the disciples do.

This is a grace I often use as I sit down to eat.

> Bless, O Lord,
> this food for our use,
> ourselves to your service,
> and make us ever mindful
> of the needs of others.
> Amen.

6.oopm

'My body ... my blood'

While they were eating, Jesus took a loaf of bread, and after blessing it he broke it, gave it to the disciples, and said, 'Take, eat; this is my body.' Then he took a cup, and after giving thanks he gave it to them, saying, 'Drink from it, all of you; for this is my blood of the covenant, which is poured out for many for the forgiveness of sins. I tell you, I will never again drink of this fruit of the vine until that day when I drink it new with you in my Father's kingdom.' (Matthew 26.26–29)

'This is my body ... this is my blood.' Those words must have brought the conversation around the table to an end. What was he saying to them? They had heard him say 'I am the bread of life' (John 6.35), they had heard him say 'Come to me all who are thirsty' (John 7.37). But now he takes bread and breaks it, takes the cup and shares it and brings them into a new place. It wasn't that they understood at this moment what was happening, but they knew something was happening.

By the time St Paul was writing his first letter to the church in Corinth, others had realized that something had happened at that moment. Paul reflects on the Eucharist in their community and gives us an insight into what the early church was doing and how they were doing it. And at the heart of what they were doing and what they were saying were the words of Jesus from the Last Supper.

For I received from the Lord what I also handed on to you, that the Lord Jesus on the night when he was betrayed took a loaf of bread, and when he had given thanks, he broke it and said, 'This is my body that is for you. Do this in remembrance of me.' In the same way he took the cup also, after supper, saying, 'This cup is the new covenant in my blood. Do this, as often as you drink it, in remembrance of me.' For as often as you eat this bread and drink the cup, you proclaim the Lord's death until he comes. (1 Corinthians 11.23–26)

It doesn't matter how 'high' or 'low' our church tradition, it doesn't matter what our theology of the Eucharist is, it doesn't matter how we understand the presence of Jesus in the eucharistic species, we know that when we hear these words we hear words echoing through the centuries, echoing from the Upper Room to the room where our community of faith is gathered and is breaking bread. Time is concertinaed and we are at the one table, at the one meal, with the one Lord, sharing in the one bread. As Paul says earlier in that letter:

Because there is one bread, we who are many are one body, for we all partake of the one bread. (1 Corinthians 10.17)

It is the meal of unity. The supper draws into true communion and true community with God and it finds its daily expression in the Eucharist.

This is the collect for the feast of Corpus Christi, the day on which the church gives thanks for the gift of Holy Communion. The origins of the prayer lie in the writings of St Thomas Aquinas.

> Lord Jesus Christ,
> we thank you that in this wonderful sacrament
> you have given us the memorial of your passion:
> grant us so to reverence the sacred mysteries
> of your body and blood
> that we may know within ourselves
> and show forth in our lives
> the fruits of your redemption;
> for you are alive and reign with the Father
> in the unity of the Holy Spirit,
> one God, now and for ever.
> Amen.[7]

7.00pm

Too posh to wash?

During supper Jesus, knowing that the Father had given all things into his hands, and that he had come from God and was going to God, got up from the table, took off his outer robe, and tied a towel around himself. Then he poured water into a basin and began to wash the disciples' feet and to wipe them with the towel that was tied around him. He came to Simon Peter, who said to him, 'Lord, are you going to wash my feet?' Jesus answered, 'You do not know now what I am doing, but later you will understand.' Peter said to him, 'You will never wash my feet.' Jesus answered, 'Unless I wash you, you have no share with me.' Simon Peter said to him, 'Lord, not my feet only but also my hands and my head!' Jesus said to him, 'One who has bathed does not need to wash, except for the feet, but is entirely clean. And you are clean, though not all of you.' For he knew who was to betray him; for this reason he said, 'Not all of you are clean.'

*After he had washed their feet, had put on his robe,
and had returned to the table, he said to them, 'Do you
know what I have done to you? You call me Teacher and
Lord – and you are right, for that is what I am. So if I,
your Lord and Teacher, have washed your feet, you also
ought to wash one another's feet. For I have set you an
example, that you also should do as I have done to you.
Very truly, I tell you, servants are not greater than their
master, nor are messengers greater than the one who
sent them. If you know these things, you are blessed if
you do them. I am not speaking of all of you; I know
whom I have chosen. But it is to fulfil the scripture,
"The one who ate my bread has lifted his heel against
me." I tell you this now, before it occurs, so that when
it does occur, you may believe that I am he. Very truly,
I tell you, whoever receives one whom I send receives
me; and whoever receives me receives him who sent me.'*
(John 13.3–20)

Every office has them; every home has them – people who
are too 'posh to wash', who are happy to dump their
used coffee mug in the sink and allow someone else to
wash it up. Something had gone wrong on this evening. It
might have been the stress of the whole week, it may have
been not quite knowing what was happening, it might
have been that the room, though all set up, didn't have a
servant there to do it. But however it happened, there was
no provision made for washing their feet as they came in
off the dusty streets and took their place at the table.

If you have a bunch of people who crave the seats at the left
and right hands of Jesus in the kingdom then I guess they
are 'too posh to wash'. Jesus notices – he notices everything.
So it is he who gets up, takes off his outer garment and

kneels and washes their feet. Graham Kendrick wrote that well-loved hymn, 'Servant King', and that is what we now see in the Upper Room.

And of course they are mortified. Peter, as ever, is the one who has to make the loudest noise, objecting to what Jesus is doing. But their lack of thought, their lack of humility has been used by Jesus to teach us all a lesson.

In our office kitchen in the cathedral we have a sign that says:

> *This may be a community where other people wash your feet but you're still expected to do your own washing up!*

Jesus teaches us that none of us is 'too posh to wash', to take our part in life, to serve and to be served, to give and to receive. Remember that when you next leave your cup for someone else to deal with, remember that when you next pass a beggar in the street.

> Teach us, good Lord,
> to serve you as you deserve,
> to give and not to count the cost,
> to fight and not to heed the wounds,
> to toil and not to seek for rest,
> to labour and not to ask for any reward,
> save that of knowing that we do your will.
> Amen.
> (St Ignatius Loyola)

8.oopm

And it was night

After saying this Jesus was troubled in spirit, and declared, 'Very truly, I tell you, one of you will betray me.' The disciples looked at one another, uncertain of whom he was speaking. One of his disciples – the one whom Jesus loved – was reclining next to him; Simon Peter therefore motioned to him to ask Jesus of whom he was speaking. So while reclining next to Jesus, he asked him, 'Lord, who is it?' Jesus answered, 'It is the one to whom I give this piece of bread when I have dipped it in the dish.' So when he had dipped the piece of bread, he gave it to Judas son of Simon Iscariot. After he received the piece of bread, Satan entered into him. Jesus said to him, 'Do quickly what you are going to do.' Now no one at the table knew why he said this to him. Some thought that, because Judas had the common purse, Jesus was telling him, 'Buy what we need for the festival'; or, that he should give something to the poor. So, after receiving the piece of bread, he immediately went out. And it was night. (John 13.21–30)

I don't often remember the impact of a sermon but I do remember one in particular. I was only young, in the choir of our parish church in Leicester and it was Maundy Thursday and the vicar was preaching. He took for his text, 'And it was night'. He explained in such a powerful way that Judas needed the cloak of darkness to do his evil deed, but he also said that the darkness John speaks of was nothing to do with a lack of light. It was more than that, it was the darkness that humanity had brought in extinguishing the light of Christ through evil actions. Whenever I hear those four words, 'And it was night', I think of the cloak of darkness and how by my actions I extinguish that divine light.

Of course rhetorically he was right, but theologically he was wrong. We can never extinguish the light of Christ, but we can seek the darkness for our evil deeds.

May I walk in the light, Lord,
and not stumble in the darkness.
Amen.

8.30pm

Easy to say ...

> *Then Jesus said to them, 'You will all become deserters*
> *because of me this night; for it is written,*
> * "I will strike the shepherd,*
> * and the sheep of the flock will be scattered."*
> *But after I am raised up, I will go ahead of you to*
> *Galilee.' Peter said to him, 'Though all become deserters*
> *because of you, I will never desert you.' Jesus said to*
> *him, 'Truly I tell you, this very night, before the cock*
> *crows, you will deny me three times.' Peter said to him,*
> *'Even though I must die with you, I will not deny you.'*
> *And so said all the disciples.* (Matthew 26.31–35)

Be careful what you say; your words will find you out.
Peter was full of good intentions but, as Jesus will say
to them all, 'the spirit indeed is willing, but the flesh is
weak' (Matthew 26.41). It seemed to apply to Peter more
than the others. 'I will not deny you.' Sometimes it takes
a while for our words and our promises and our lack of
sincerity to find us out. It would all come home to roost
this evening for Peter – before the cock would crow.

MAUNDY THURSDAY

Let the words of my mouth and the meditation of
   my heart
be acceptable to you,
O Lord, my rock and my redeemer.
(Psalm 19.14)

8.45pm

Get real

Jesus said to the disciples, 'When I sent you out without a purse, bag, or sandals, did you lack anything?' They said, 'No, not a thing.' He said to them, 'But now, the one who has a purse must take it, and likewise a bag. And the one who has no sword must sell his cloak and buy one. For I tell you, this scripture must be fulfilled in me, "And he was counted among the lawless"; and indeed what is written about me is being fulfilled.' They said, 'Lord, look, here are two swords.' He replied, 'It is enough.'

He came out and went, as was his custom, to the Mount of Olives; and the disciples followed him. (Luke 22.35–39)

In the musical *Joseph and his Amazing Technicolor Dreamcoat* there is a song in which the brothers remember the good old days in Canaan. Days of endless golden summers and fields of clover, of mild winters and strolling down boulevards without a care. But now those Canaan days are gone, replaced by lifeless fields and bitter wine, as the brothers ask themselves: 'Where have they gone, where did they go?'[8] It's an amusing song, sung in 'Allo, allo' French accents. These verses from Luke remind me of this, though. Jesus is saying to the disciples: 'You remember when it was easy, when we wanted for nothing, those days are over; wake up to reality.' The talk of swords is ironic, of course, but irony is always lost on the disciples – hence the 'It is enough' means not that two swords is enough but that Jesus can't stand any more of their dullness and so he goes and they follow, into another world of the hunter and the hunted.

We can bask in days of ease and former glory or 'wake up and smell the coffee'. Jesus calls us to live in the world as it is, not in the world we imagine it is, and to change the world into what he desires it to be, where none are in want and the poor are rich and the rich are generous.

> Open my eyes, Lord,
> to the world around;
> open my heart, Lord,
> to love
> as you love us.
> Amen.

9.00pm

Into the garden

Then Jesus went with them to a place called Gethsemane; and he said to his disciples, 'Sit here while I go over there and pray.' He took with him Peter and the two sons of Zebedee, and began to be grieved and agitated. Then he said to them, 'I am deeply grieved, even to death; remain here, and stay awake with me.' And going a little farther, he threw himself on the ground and prayed, 'My Father, if it is possible, let this cup pass from me; yet not what I want but what you want.' (Matthew 26.36–39)

It is in these moments that we see Jesus in all his humanity: '... if it is possible ...' How often have I wanted the cup to pass me by, to not have to do what I most fear, which will be so costly. But I cannot avoid it – well, only by running away from my responsibilities. Jesus has nowhere to run.

There will be those this evening facing a cup from which they would rather not drink. Jesus is with them in their agony because, as the writer of the Letter to the Hebrews tells us:

Because he himself was tested by what he suffered, he is able to help those who are being tested. (Hebrews 2.18)

Be present, O merciful God,
and protect us through the silent hours of this night,
so that we who are wearied
by the changes and chances of this fleeting world,
may rest upon your eternal changelessness;
through Jesus Christ our Lord.
Amen.[9]

9.15pm

Watch over me

Then an angel from heaven appeared to him and gave him strength. In his anguish he prayed more earnestly, and his sweat became like great drops of blood falling down on the ground. (Luke 22.43–44)

I sometimes wake in the night gripped by fear or anxiety. It is normally about nothing – it just looks worse than it is at night. But the night fears, the sweats, the quickened heart beat – well, this is what Jesus was going through. Luke tells us that an angel, a messenger from God, appears to him to give him strength. The angels had been before, in the wilderness, at the beginning of his ministry as the forty days in the wilderness were ending. Matthew writes: '… and suddenly angels came and waited on him' (Matthew 4.11b). Now they were back as that ministry seems to be drawing to its dramatic, earth-shattering conclusion.

In those times of my own anxiety, what do I do? Worry more or pray, allow God to calm my fears, allow my quickened heart to quieten in the 'peace of God which passes all understanding'? I pray for those going through anxiety this evening, for whatever reason, that an angel will minister to them, and that I may allow God's messengers – whomsoever they may be – to minister to me.

This prayer may be 'child-like' but it is memorable for the night-time.

> Angel of God, my Guardian dear,
> to whom His love commits me here,
> ever this night be at my side,
> to light and guard, to rule and guide.
> Amen.

9.30pm

The silence is broken

*Then he came to the disciples and found them sleeping;
and he said to Peter, 'So, could you not stay awake with
me one hour? Stay awake and pray that you may not
come into the time of trial; the spirit indeed is willing,
but the flesh is weak.' Again he went away for the second
time and prayed, 'My Father, if this cannot pass unless
I drink it, your will be done.' Again he came and found
them sleeping, for their eyes were heavy. So leaving them
again, he went away and prayed for the third time, saying
the same words. Then he came to the disciples and said
to them, 'Are you still sleeping and taking your rest? See,
the hour is at hand, and the Son of Man is betrayed into
the hands of sinners. Get up, let us be going. See, my
betrayer is at hand.'* (Matthew 26.40–46)

They were exhausted and, despite being woken by Jesus
and admonished by him on a number of occasions as the
evening wore on, it was too much. They were meant to
be with him, but they had already left him, as they would
physically leave him in just a few moments.

They looked up – through the trees they could see the light of approaching torches and they could hear the noise of a crowd, but more than that, the noise of a mob. In the glade where they were, among the olive trees, they felt as though they were surrounded. They had been called by Jesus to 'fish for people' but now they were being hunted like animals. Then the words from Jesus came, 'See, my betrayer is at hand', and they looked up not knowing what or who to expect.

Lord, have mercy.
Christ, have mercy.
Lord, have mercy.

9.45pm

The kiss

While he was still speaking, Judas, one of the twelve, arrived; with him was a large crowd with swords and clubs, from the chief priests and the elders of the people. Now the betrayer had given them a sign, saying, 'The one I will kiss is the man; arrest him.' At once he came up to Jesus and said, 'Greetings, Rabbi!' and kissed him. Jesus said to him, 'Friend, do what you are here to do.' Then they came and laid hands on Jesus and arrested him. Suddenly, one of those with Jesus put his hand on his sword, drew it, and struck the slave of the high priest, cutting off his ear. Then Jesus said to him, 'Put your sword back into its place; for all who take the sword will perish by the sword. Do you think that I cannot appeal to my Father, and he will at once send me more than twelve legions of angels? But how then would the scriptures be fulfilled, which say it must happen in this way?' At that hour Jesus said to the crowds, 'Have you come out with swords and clubs to arrest me as though I were a bandit? Day after day I sat in the temple teach-

ing, and you did not arrest me. But all this has taken place, so that the scriptures of the prophets may be fulfilled.' Then all the disciples deserted him and fled. (Matthew 26.47–56)

Anne Frank and her family were hiding in the sealed-off rooms in the office building that was prepared for them by their friends. For four years they were there, supplied with all they needed to survive on. Then on 4 August 1944 members of the Nazi Security Service and Dutch policemen arrived, broke their way in and arrested them. Someone had betrayed them. They were taken off to a concentration camp and killed. There has been a great deal of speculation about who the betrayer was – but it remains unsolved.

But Jesus knew his betrayer, and the disciples looked on in horror as Judas walked out of the crowd and kissed Jesus, and the soldiers descended on him. A kiss. It was the worst thing he could have done. A kiss.

There is a beautiful statue of Our Lady and the child Jesus in the chapel of the Community of St Mary the Virgin, Wantage. The statue was carved by Mother Maribel CSMV and shows the Holy Mother gently kissing the forehead of her child. It is a beautiful kiss of love – so different from this kiss of betrayal that Judas now inflicts on Jesus. The sign of love, the sign of devotion is scorned as the kiss becomes the sign, subverts the sign. But nothing will be as it seems this evening, for the forces of darkness are at work.

Almighty Father,
look with mercy on this your family
for which our Lord Jesus Christ was content to
    be betrayed
and given up into the hands of sinners
and to suffer death upon the cross;
who is alive and glorified with you and the Holy Spirit,
one God, now and for ever.
Amen.[10]

9.50pm

Loss of innocence

A certain young man was following him, wearing nothing but a linen cloth. They caught hold of him, but he left the linen cloth and ran off naked. (Mark 14.51–52)

We don't know who this young man was. Some people think it was Mark himself – no other Evangelist mentions this trivial detail. But that is what life is made up of to such a huge extent – trivial, inconsequential details. But this young boy must have been petrified as his clothes were ripped from him and he fled for his life. He had not seen anything like this.

My heart grieves for children caught up in the things that they should never see, never be involved in. The famous photograph taken by the photographer Nick Ut, of the little girl, Phan Thị Kim Phúc, fleeing the napalm attack in Vietnam, is seared into my memory as the horrors were seared into her skin. The boy in the garden escaped with his life and only his dignity had been hurt – but these children lose everything including, and most precious of all, their innocence.

> God, Mother, Father,
> hear the cry of your children
> who lose their innocence
> through war, abuse, neglect;
> hold them and love them.
> Amen.

10.30pm

Arrested

Those who had arrested Jesus took him to Caiaphas the high priest, in whose house the scribes and the elders had gathered. But Peter was following him at a distance, as far as the courtyard of the high priest; and going inside, he sat with the guards in order to see how this would end. Now the chief priests and the whole council were looking for false testimony against Jesus so that they might put him to death, but they found none, though many false witnesses came forward. At last two came forward and said, 'This fellow said, "I am able to destroy the temple of God and to build it in three days."' The high priest stood up and said, 'Have you no answer? What is it that they testify against you?' But Jesus was silent. Then the high priest said to him, 'I put you under oath before the living God, tell us if you are the Messiah, the Son of God.' Jesus said to him, 'You have said so. But I tell you,

> *From now on you will see the Son of Man*
> *seated at the right hand of Power*
> *and coming on the clouds of heaven.'*

Then the high priest tore his clothes and said, 'He has blasphemed! Why do we still need witnesses? You have now heard his blasphemy. What is your verdict?' They answered, 'He deserves death.' Then they spat in his face and struck him; and some slapped him, saying, 'Prophesy to us, you Messiah! Who is it that struck you?' (Matthew 26.57–68)

So his words come back to him. At the beginning of the week he made this prophecy about the temple. But, as we know, he was speaking of his body. Others though had been listening, noting his words, biding their time until his words could be turned back on him. And now it happens and the high priest is delighted. Caiaphas needed a bit of evidence on which to hang the rest of the accusations, on which to hang the man. And the verdict came quickly: 'He deserves death.'

Let the groans of the prisoners come before you;
according to your great power preserve those
   doomed to die.
(Psalm 79.11)

10.45pm

The cock crows

Now Peter was sitting outside in the courtyard. A servant-girl came to him and said, 'You also were with Jesus the Galilean.' But he denied it before all of them, saying, 'I do not know what you are talking about.' When he went out to the porch, another servant-girl saw him, and she said to the bystanders, 'This man was with Jesus of Nazareth.' Again he denied it with an oath, 'I do not know the man.' After a little while the bystanders came up and said to Peter, 'Certainly you are also one of them, for your accent betrays you.' Then he began to curse, and he swore an oath, 'I do not know the man!' At that moment the cock crowed. Then Peter remembered what Jesus had said: 'Before the cock crows, you will deny me three times.' And he went out and wept bitterly.
(Matthew 26.69–75)

There is a church that now stands in Jerusalem on the site of the house of the high priest. It's called St Peter in Gallicantu (the cockcrow). While Jesus was being condemned to death in the house, Peter was outside. He had followed at a distance as the soldiers took Jesus from the Garden of Gethsemane across the Kidron Valley. That was a familiar journey; they had walked part of this way each day as they made their way backwards and forwards between Bethany and Jerusalem.

But now they followed a slightly different route. The house was on Mount Sion but just outside the walls. It meant going past the Tomb of Absalom, which you can see to this day in the valley. Absalom was the son of King David, killed in battle, a traitor against his father but mourned and loved by David nevertheless. Now this true Son of David is arrested and being taken for trial and Peter knows that they want him dead.

Sitting there in the courtyard he tries to look inconspicuous – but he is a northerner down in the big city. He only has to speak to give the game away and, despite denying knowing Jesus three times, it's obvious that he is one of them, one of the band of disciples of the prisoner inside.

Then the door opens – Jesus is led out and as he passes by the cock crows and their eyes meet. Jesus doesn't need to say anything and neither does Peter.

Lord, for the many times I have denied you
in word or silence
in action or inaction,
forgive me.
Amen.

11.00pm

In the depths

Now the men who were holding Jesus began to mock him and beat him; they also blindfolded him and kept asking him, 'Prophesy! Who is it that struck you?' They kept heaping many other insults on him.
(Luke 22.63–65)

Pilgrims are taken through the church of St Peter in Gallicantu and down a series of steps deep below the level of the church and the former dwelling. They go to see a dungeon. Basically it is a hole dug out beneath the foundations of the house. There was one way in, through an opening in the top, and the prisoner would have been let down on ropes under his arms and left there in the dark. Another entrance has been cut for pilgrims and we enter this terrifying space. The lights are turned out and we stand in silence. This is probably where Jesus was on that night, having been beaten, abused by his captors – like so many prisoners. Was he terrified? He must have been. He had been praying that the cup be taken from him just a couple of hours ago and now he is here.

Out of the depths I cry to you, O LORD.
Lord, hear my voice!
Let your ears be attentive
to the voice of my supplications!
If you, O LORD, should mark iniquities,
Lord, who could stand?
But there is forgiveness with you,
so that you may be revered.
I wait for the LORD, my soul waits,
and in his word I hope;
my soul waits for the LORD
more than those who watch for the morning,
more than those who watch for the morning.
O Israel, hope in the LORD!
For with the LORD there is steadfast love,
and with him is great power to redeem.
It is he who will redeem Israel
from all its iniquities.
(Psalm 130)

Good Friday

6.00am

A new day dawns

*When morning came, all the chief priests and the elders
of the people conferred together against Jesus in order
to bring about his death. They bound him, led him away,
and handed him over to Pilate the governor.* (Matthew
27.1–2)

It is already morning, though Jesus wouldn't know – it
is so dark in the dungeon. But the stone is removed from
above him and the ropes come down and he is hauled up.
The pain is agonizing. He thinks of the prophet Jeremiah
being kept in that dried-out well and lifted up on ropes
(Jeremiah 38). They had provided for him padding to put
under his arms but there was no comfort for Jesus.

Instead, as soon as he emerged, he was tied and dragged away to see Pilate the governor and the sun was coming up.

As this new day dawns
give us the strength, Lord,
to face what it holds.
Amen.

7.00am

The unstoppable train of events

When Judas, his betrayer, saw that Jesus was condemned, he repented and brought back the thirty pieces of silver to the chief priests and the elders. He said, 'I have sinned by betraying innocent blood.' But they said, 'What is that to us? See to it yourself.' Throwing down the pieces of silver in the temple, he departed; and he went and hanged himself. But the chief priests, taking the pieces of silver, said, 'It is not lawful to put them into the treasury, since they are blood money.' After conferring together, they used them to buy the potter's field as a place to bury foreigners. For this reason that field has been called the Field of Blood to this day. Then was fulfilled what had been spoken through the prophet Jeremiah, 'And they took the thirty pieces of silver, the price of the one on whom a price had been set, on whom some of the people of Israel had set a price, and they gave them for the potter's field, as the Lord commanded me.'
(Matthew 27.3–10)

It was too late to stop what was happening. Seeing what had taken place the night before, Judas could not have slept at all. What had he done? He had to try and stop it, he had to try and rescue himself from this, he had to get rid of the money that he had taken, the price of the man he loved, the price of a kiss. And as soon as he could he goes to the chief priests. The day is just beginning but everything has ended for Judas.

They laugh at him. He did what they wanted; he played into their hands – why should they be bothered with him now? We are seeing the worst face of humanity. This is all so ugly – and Judas can take no more of it – he throws down the coins and runs out and ends it all, escapes the terror of what he has set in motion, this unstoppable nightmare that is the reality of this day.

But there will be others at the very edge today, others who are waking into a living nightmare today, others who have set in train a disastrous course of events. Lord, save them; Lord, have mercy on them; Lord, have mercy on us.

> Almighty God,
> have mercy on us,
> forgive us our sins
> and bring us to life eternal.
> Amen.

7.15am

Pontius Pilate appears

Now Jesus stood before the governor; and the governor asked him, 'Are you the King of the Jews?' Jesus said, 'You say so.' But when he was accused by the chief priests and elders, he did not answer. Then Pilate said to him, 'Do you not hear how many accusations they make against you?' But he gave him no answer, not even to a single charge, so that the governor was greatly amazed. (Matthew 27.11–14)

There is something so dignified about Jesus, standing there before Pilate. He has been brought from that dungeon under the house of Caiaphas and taken to the other side of the Temple Mount where the Antonia Fortress stood. There he was dragged before Pilate for whom this was his HQ. But he refuses to play their game, refuses to give them what they want – 'You say so.' Just three words, three defiant words.

This is the first time we meet Pontius Pilate. We will meet him quite a bit before this day ends and we will feel that we have got to know him. Instead of being a walk-on character in the Passion, a bit-player on the margins, this Roman official will become part of history and each Sunday Christians around the world will mention his name as they say 'suffered under Pontius Pilate ...', as they recite the Creed. He thought he was going to an obscure and fractious posting. He was right about the latter – but he has not been lost in obscurity, not at all. We never know what role will be asked of us in life.

I don't know what you will ask of me today, Lord.
I only ask that you will give me the strength to do it.
Amen.

7.30am

Mistaken identity?

Now at the festival the governor was accustomed to release a prisoner for the crowd, anyone whom they wanted. At that time they had a notorious prisoner, called Jesus Barabbas. So after they had gathered, Pilate said to them, 'Whom do you want me to release for you, Jesus Barabbas or Jesus who is called the Messiah?' For he realized that it was out of jealousy that they had handed him over. While he was sitting on the judgement seat, his wife sent word to him, 'Have nothing to do with that innocent man, for today I have suffered a great deal because of a dream about him.' Now the chief priests and the elders persuaded the crowds to ask for Barabbas and to have Jesus killed. The governor again said to them, 'Which of the two do you want me to release for you?' And they said, 'Barabbas.' Pilate said to them, 'Then what should I do with Jesus who is called the Messiah?' All of them said, 'Let him be crucified!' Then he asked, 'Why, what evil has he done?' But they shouted all the more, 'Let him be crucified!'
(Matthew 27.15–23)

Are you surprised? Are you confused? The mob is given a choice – free Jesus or free Jesus Barabbas. We know the name Barabbas, but did you know that he was also called Jesus and did you realize that his surname means 'son of the father'? (Remember when Jesus says 'Abba, Father'.) So, make your choice between Jesus who has described himself as son of the Father and Jesus who is known as 'son of the father'.

The early church father Origen was so troubled by the fact that his copies of the gospels gave Barabbas' name as 'Jesus Barabbas' that he declared that since it was impossible this bandit could have had such a holy name, 'Jesus' must have been added to Barabbas' name by a heretic. It is highly likely that later scribes, copying the passage, removed the name 'Jesus' from 'Jesus Barabbas' to avoid dishonour to the name of Jesus the Messiah. Only with further scholarship has this been corrected. But it makes it all very confusing and very disturbing. Was there an even greater miscarriage of justice going on?

> For all accused of a crime they have not committed,
> for all on remand,
> for all unjustly imprisoned:
> Lord, in your mercy,
> hear our prayer.

7.45 am

I wash my hands of you

So when Pilate saw that he could do nothing, but rather that a riot was beginning, he took some water and washed his hands before the crowd, saying, 'I am innocent of this man's blood; see to it yourselves.' Then the people as a whole answered, 'His blood be on us and on our children!' So he released Barabbas for them; and after flogging Jesus, he handed him over to be crucified. (Matthew 27.24–26)

Was he just a coward? His wife had been out to tell him that she had had a dream that night and that he was to have nothing to do with this man before him. Whether he has listened to his wife or not he decides enough is enough. One thing he had to do was keep the peace on this edge of the empire. It looked like there would be a riot – give them what they want, if it will keep the peace.

So a bowl is brought and he washes his hands of the problem, washes his hands of the man, washes his hands and gives Jesus into their hands.

As often as I want to wash my hands of something the truth is I can't – but it is tempting.

Lord, make me strong enough
to do the right thing
and not to wash my hands
of my responsibilities.
Amen.

8.00am

The beast within

Then the soldiers of the governor took Jesus into the governor's headquarters, and they gathered the whole cohort around him. They stripped him and put a scarlet robe on him, and after twisting some thorns into a crown, they put it on his head. They put a reed in his right hand and knelt before him and mocked him, saying, 'Hail, King of the Jews!' They spat on him, and took the reed and struck him on the head. After mocking him, they stripped him of the robe and put his own clothes on him. Then they led him away to crucify him. (Matthew 27.27–31)

I remember when I was at school reading *The Lord of the Flies* by William Golding and being shocked by the realization of how dreadful we can so easily be when we allow ourselves to respond to our baser instincts. If we do, terrible things can happen. In the book Golding writes:

Ralph wept for the end of innocence, the darkness of man's heart, and the fall through the air of the true, wise friend called Piggy.[11]

As the soldiers abuse, mock, torture Jesus we see the beast that is within us unleashed, and we weep for the end of innocence. And 'the beast' as Golding describes it still roams the earth as other prisoners are abused, mocked, ill-treated, as women are routinely raped in times of war, as people are trafficked, as children are abused.

Jesus wears the crown of thorns and the thorns still dig deep into humanity's brow.

> O sacred head, sore wounded,
> defiled and put to scorn;
> O kingly head surrounded
> with mocking crown of thorn:
> What sorrow mars thy grandeur?
> Can death thy bloom deflower?
> O countenance whose splendour
> the hosts of heaven adore![12]

8.15am

Take up thy cross

They compelled a passer-by, who was coming in from the country, to carry his cross; it was Simon of Cyrene, the father of Alexander and Rufus. (Mark 15.21)

Cyrene was a Greek town in what we now know as Libya. It also had a Jewish colony. So it may well have been that Simon, a North African Jew, had made the journey to Jerusalem for the festival of the Passover and just happened to be in the wrong place at the wrong time.

Jesus was exhausted, continual beatings, sleep deprivation, questioning, abuse – we are still familiar with the way in which prisoners can be treated even by regimes of which much better should be expected. Now he was meant to carry his cross from the Antonia Fortress to outside the city wall and the Place of the Skull. What he would have been carrying would have been the crossbar on to which he would be nailed and then hauled up the upright that was already in place and which would be used for every prisoner.

Pilgrims to Jerusalem, walking the Via Dolorosa, have the experience of carrying the cross between the fourteen stations that mark the way that Jesus walked. It is a tough thing to do – physically and emotionally – and it is normal for the cross to be shared, two bearing it at one time and swopping at various points in the journey with others eager to do this.

There was no one eager to do it for Jesus. Simon had to be compelled, perhaps with a lash, to do this ignominious act. But later he must have realized what he had done and must have become a Christian, perhaps the first to be converted on the Way of the Cross.

Why do I say this? Well, Mark in his Gospel mentions Simon's sons, Alexander and Rufus. Mark was writing his Gospel for the Christian community in Rome. To bother to mention these two names must have meant that it was significant for those first readers. They must have known them; they must have been part of their community. Simon carries the cross for Jesus and then carries the cross for the rest of his life as a Christian and brings his family with him.

> 'Take up thy cross,' the Saviour said,
> 'If thou wouldst My disciple be;
> Deny thyself, the world forsake,
> And humbly follow after Me.'
> Take up thy cross, let not its weight
> Fill thy weak spirit with alarm;
> His strength shall bear thy spirit up,
> And brace thy heart and nerve thine arm.
> Take up thy cross, nor heed the shame,
> Nor let thy foolish pride rebel;

Thy Lord for thee the cross endured,
And saved thy soul from death and hell.
Take up thy cross then in His strength,
And calmly sin's wild deluge brave,
'Twill guide thee to a better home,
It points to glory o'er the grave.
Take up thy cross and follow Christ,
Nor think 'til death to lay it down;
For only those who bear the cross
May hope to wear the glorious crown.
To Thee, great Lord, the One in Three,
All praise forevermore ascend:
O grant us in our home to see
The heavenly life that knows no end.[13]

8.30am

Are these tears real?

A great number of the people followed him, and among them were women who were beating their breasts and wailing for him. But Jesus turned to them and said, 'Daughters of Jerusalem, do not weep for me, but weep for yourselves and for your children. For the days are surely coming when they will say, "Blessed are the barren, and the wombs that never bore, and the breasts that never nursed." Then they will begin to say to the mountains, "Fall on us"; and to the hills, "Cover us." For if they do this when the wood is green, what will happen when it is dry?' (Luke 23.27–31)

Lament is a powerful, passionate response to grief and this is what we see in these women who are standing, wailing as the prisoner passes by. Some suggest that they may have been professional 'wailers' so that what we have here are 'crocodile tears'. If that is true that may be why Jesus turns and speaks to them. He calls on them to weep heartfelt tears, to express real lament for themselves and their children, not for him. He ends what he says with an enigmatic saying which some people suggest we don't really understand. It's worth thinking about. Perhaps it simply means, 'If innocence meets such a fate, what will be in store for the guilty?'

But this is the wonderful thing about scripture – the meaning of so much is not obvious and it is good to pray about it and let it take root in us. This is a great prayer for thinking about this.

> Blessed Lord,
> who caused all holy Scriptures to be written for
>   our learning:
> help us so to hear them,
> to read, mark, learn and inwardly digest them
> that, through patience, and the comfort of your
>   holy word,
> we may embrace and for ever hold fast
> the hope of everlasting life,
> which you have given us in our Saviour Jesus Christ.
> Amen.[14]

8.45 am

An escape route

And when they came to a place called Golgotha (which means Place of a Skull), they offered him wine to drink, mixed with gall; but when he tasted it, he would not drink it. (Matthew 27.33–34)

It was to dull the pain, this drink they offered him. But he didn't want it. Drink, drugs, shopping, gambling, pornography, sex – we can resort to so many things to dull the pain of our lives, to blur our vision of reality and to take us to a place we would rather be than the place that we are. Even in the midst of a horrible reality, Jesus resists what is offered to him. What he is going through is real and he stays with it.

> When I am tempted to blur reality,
> to dull the pain,
> to escape what's happening,
> Lord, give me the courage
> to stay with it.
> Amen.

9.00am

The clock starts ticking

It was nine o'clock in the morning when they crucified him. The inscription of the charge against him read, 'The King of the Jews.' (Mark 15.25–26)

The clock starts ticking. The nails have been driven in, the cross beam raised with Jesus attached, raised so that all can see him, so that all can see his agony. The clock starts ticking and time begins to take on a different pace, for him, for the watchers, for the witnesses, for us. 'How long, O Lord, how long?' (cf. Psalm 13.1). The clock starts ticking and Jesus hangs there.

> Lord of time and of eternity,
> sustain those for whom time will go slowly today;
> those watching a loved one in pain,
> those waiting for important news,
> those with time but nothing to do with it,
> for us, watching, waiting with Jesus.
> Amen.

10.00am

... and ticking ...

> *Then two bandits were crucified with him, one on his*
> *right and one on his left. Those who passed by derided*
> *him, shaking their heads and saying, 'You who would*
> *destroy the temple and build it in three days, save your-*
> *self! If you are the Son of God, come down from the*
> *cross.' In the same way the chief priests also, along with*
> *the scribes and elders, were mocking him, saying, 'He*
> *saved others; he cannot save himself. He is the King of*
> *Israel; let him come down from the cross now, and we*
> *will believe in him. He trusts in God; let God deliver*
> *him now, if he wants to; for he said, "I am God's Son."'*
> *The bandits who were crucified with him also taunted*
> *him in the same way.* (Matthew 27.38–44)

It has been an hour since the nails were driven in and he was
raised for all to see. The pain is unbearable, breathing is
agonizing. But even this is not torture enough. The crowds
beneath him, even those who are crucified alongside him,
batter him with words and insults.

We used to sing in the playground

Sticks and stones will break my bones
But words will never harm me.

It's true of course, but words can get under our skin and we can believe what others say about us; words can be like darts in the side, arrows in the heart. St James warns us about the tongue:

The tongue is a fire. The tongue is placed among our members as a world of iniquity; it stains the whole body, sets on fire the cycle of nature, and is itself set on fire by hell. (James 3.6)

The words were like more nails being driven home, and the clock kept ticking.

Keep your tongue from evil,
and your lips from speaking deceit.
(Psalm 34.13)

11.00am

... and ticking ...

> *One of the criminals who were hanged there kept derid-ing him and saying, 'Are you not the Messiah? Save yourself and us!' But the other rebuked him, saying, 'Do you not fear God, since you are under the same sentence of condemnation? And we indeed have been condemned justly, for we are getting what we deserve for our deeds, but this man has done nothing wrong.' Then he said, 'Jesus, remember me when you come into your kingdom.' He replied, 'Truly I tell you, today you will be with me in Paradise.'* (Luke 23.39–43)

It has been two hours since the nails were driven in and he was raised for all to see. The two criminals crucified with Jesus have had some time to think about what is happening. They've heard the way in which the crowds were reacting to the one between them, this one called 'The King of Jews' on the accusation above his head.

But one keeps on jeering, deriding Jesus. Even though he is in pain he can't stop himself going for Jesus. But the other;

he was throwing insults, but gradually he stopped. Now he rebukes the other guy and from his place of pain comes out with a declaration of faith:

'Jesus, remember me when you come into your kingdom.'

And Jesus replies:

'Today you will be with me in Paradise.'

It is a deeply moving moment. It reminds me that people react so differently to the same experience. Some can never get over their anger and want to hurl abuse at whomever, whatever they can. Others will allow themselves to be changed and peace enters their heart. Even on the cross someone is converted, but not everyone will be.

And the clock kept ticking.

Jesus, remember me when you come into your kingdom. Amen.

11.15am

The robe

When the soldiers had crucified Jesus, they took his clothes and divided them into four parts, one for each soldier. They also took his tunic; now the tunic was seamless, woven in one piece from the top. So they said to one another, 'Let us not tear it, but cast lots for it to see who will get it.' This was to fulfil what the scripture says,

*   'They divided my clothes among themselves,*
*   and for my clothing they cast lots.'*
And that is what the soldiers did. (John 19.23–25)

It wasn't the best job to have, watching, waiting while a prisoner died. The clock ticked but time dragged. So a game of dice was good and so was dividing up the spoils. But even these rough and ready soldiers recognized a good garment when they saw one. If they ripped it into four – well, that would be pointless. So the dice came in handy.

The Greek is helpful here. The word translated as 'clothes' means 'the undergarments'. But the word translated as 'tunic' is *khitōn*, a tunic or a coat, an outer garment. The robe has been the subject of devotion and legend. It featured in the 1953 film *The Robe* with Richard Burton and Jean Simmons, and the strongest tradition is that it was discovered by St Helena, the mother of Constantine, in 327 or 328 and was given to the monastery at Trier, where it remains. Other robes are also said to exist.

As with all relics the important thing is not the object but the faith and devotion it engenders. Scripture says there was a robe; it may still exist, but the more important thing is that the one who wore it hung there as people fought over it. He is the one in whom we place our faith.

And the clock kept ticking.

At baptism, as the newly baptized is wrapped in a white robe, the priest says:

> You have been clothed with Christ.
> As many as are baptized into Christ have put on Christ.[15]

Make of it your own prayer.

11.30am

Behold your mother

> *Meanwhile, standing near the cross of Jesus were his mother, and his mother's sister, Mary the wife of Clopas, and Mary Magdalene. When Jesus saw his mother and the disciple whom he loved standing beside her, he said to his mother, 'Woman, here is your son.' Then he said to the disciple, 'Here is your mother.' And from that hour the disciple took her into his own home.*
> (John 19.25–27)

This moment has inspired so much art, so much devotion, so much prayer. The most powerful is the thirteenth-century Latin Sequence (a form of liturgical hymn) called the Stabat Mater. It has been set to music by so many composers. My favourite is that by Giovanni Battista Pergolesi, composed in 1736 in the final weeks of his life. It captures the pain and the dignity of the woman who has to go through what no woman or man should, watching their child die.

And the clock kept ticking.

At the cross her station keeping,
stood the mournful mother weeping,
close to Jesus at the last,
Through her soul, of joy bereavèd,
bowed with anguish, deeply grievèd,
now at length the sword hath passed.
O, that blessed one, grief-laden,
blessed Mother, blessed Maiden,
Mother of the all-holy One;
O that silent, ceaseless mourning,
O those dim eyes, never turning
from that wondrous, suffering Son.
Who, on Christ's dear mother gazing,
in her trouble so amazing,
born of woman, would not weep?
Who, on Christ's dear Mother thinking,
such a cup of sorrow drinking,
would not share her sorrows deep?
For his people's sins, in anguish,
there she saw the victim languish,
bleed in torments, bleed and die.
Saw the Lord's anointed taken,
saw her Child in death forsaken,
heard his last expiring cry.
In the passion of my Maker,
be my sinful soul partaker,
may I bear with her my part;
of his passion bear the token,
in a spirit bowed and broken
bear his death within my heart.
May his wounds both wound and heal me,
he enkindle, cleanse, and heal me,
be his cross my hope and stay.

May he, when the mountains quiver,
from that flame which burns for ever
shield me on the judgment day.
Jesus, may thy cross defend me,
and thy saving death befriend me,
cherished by thy deathless grace:
when to dust my dust returneth,
grant a soul that to thee yearneth
in thy paradise a place.[16]

12.00 noon

... and ticking ...

> *It was now about noon, and darkness came over the whole land until three in the afternoon, while the sun's light failed; and the curtain of the temple was torn in two.* (Luke 23.44–45)

It has been three hours since the nails were driven in and he was raised for all to see. There are three more hours to go, three more hours of agony, three more hours in which he suppresses the screams, in which he fights for breath, in which his blood flows. Three more hours for his mother to watch him, three more hours for the women to keep vigil, three more hours for John to stand in horror, three more hours for the crowds to jeer, three more hours for the solders to wait. And the universe waits, and heaven waits and we wait.

And the clock kept ticking.

A prayer of St Richard of Chichester.

Thanks be to thee, my Lord Jesus Christ,
For all the benefits which thou hast given to me,
For all the pains and insults which thou hast borne
    for me.
O most merciful redeemer, friend and brother,
May I know thee more clearly
Love thee more dearly,
And follow thee more nearly,
Day by day.
Amen.

2.50pm

'My God, my God ...'

> *And about three o'clock Jesus cried with a loud voice,*
> *'Eli, Eli, lema sabachthani?' that is, 'My God, my God,*
> *why have you forsaken me?' When some of the bystand-*
> *ers heard it, they said, 'This man is calling for Elijah.'*
> *At once one of them ran and got a sponge, filled it with*
> *sour wine, put it on a stick, and gave it to him to drink.*
> *But the others said, 'Wait, let us see whether Elijah will*
> *come to save him.'* (Matthew 27.46–49)

The agonizing silence that has fallen on them as the skies
have darkened in the middle of the day, the sense of fore-
boding that has enveloped them; it is all shattered as Jesus
cries out from the cross. Does he feel that God has aban-
doned him, or is he saying one of the psalms that he said
at home and in the synagogue? Perhaps it is a bit of both.

As we read Psalm 22, so much of it speaks to us of what
we are witnessing now.

And the clock kept ticking.

My God, my God, why have you forsaken me?
Why are you so far from helping me, from the words
   of my groaning?
O my God, I cry by day, but you do not answer;
and by night, but find no rest.
Yet you are holy,
enthroned on the praises of Israel.
In you our ancestors trusted;
they trusted, and you delivered them.
To you they cried, and were saved;
in you they trusted, and were not put to shame.
But I am a worm, and not human;
scorned by others, and despised by the people.
All who see me mock at me;
they make mouths at me, they shake their heads;
'Commit your cause to the LORD; let him deliver –
let him rescue the one in whom he delights!'
Yet it was you who took me from the womb;
you kept me safe on my mother's breast.
On you I was cast from my birth,
and since my mother bore me you have been my God.
Do not be far from me,
for trouble is near
and there is no one to help.
Many bulls encircle me,
strong bulls of Bashan surround me;
they open wide their mouths at me,
like a ravening and roaring lion.
I am poured out like water,
and all my bones are out of joint;
my heart is like wax;
it is melted within my breast;
my mouth is dried up like a potsherd,

and my tongue sticks to my jaws;
you lay me in the dust of death.
For dogs are all around me;
a company of evildoers encircles me.
My hands and feet have shrivelled;
I can count all my bones.
They stare and gloat over me;
they divide my clothes among themselves,
and for my clothing they cast lots.
But you, O LORD, do not be far away!
O my help, come quickly to my aid!
Deliver my soul from the sword,
my life from the power of the dog!
Save me from the mouth of the lion!
From the horns of the wild oxen you have rescued me.
I will tell of your name to my brothers and sisters;
in the midst of the congregation I will praise you:
You who fear the LORD, praise him!
All you offspring of Jacob, glorify him;
stand in awe of him, all you offspring of Israel!
For he did not despise or abhor
the affliction of the afflicted;
he did not hide his face from me,
but heard when I cried to him.
From you comes my praise in the great congregation;
my vows I will pay before those who fear him.
The poor shall eat and be satisfied;
those who seek him shall praise the LORD.
May your hearts live for ever!
All the ends of the earth shall remember
and turn to the LORD;
and all the families of the nations
shall worship before him.

For dominion belongs to the LORD,
and he rules over the nations.
To him, indeed, shall all who sleep in the earth bow
   down;
before him shall bow all who go down to the dust,
and I shall live for him.
Posterity will serve him;
future generations will be told about the Lord,
and proclaim his deliverance to a people yet unborn,
saying that he has done it.
(Psalm 22)

3.00pm

... and stops

After this, when Jesus knew that all was now finished, he said (in order to fulfil the scripture), 'I am thirsty.' A jar full of sour wine was standing there. So they put a sponge full of the wine on a branch of hyssop and held it to his mouth. When Jesus had received the wine, he said, 'It is finished.' Then he bowed his head and gave up his spirit. (John 19.28–30)

The clock stops, the universe stops, time itself stops, history seems to crumple. God is dead. 'It is finished.'

> Lord, have mercy upon us
> and forgive us,
> for we know not what we do.

3.15pm

Emerging from the nightmare

> *And when all the crowds who had gathered there for this spectacle saw what had taken place, they returned home, beating their breasts. But all his acquaintances, including the women who had followed him from Galilee, stood at a distance, watching these things.*
> (Luke 23.48–49)

For most of the people who were there the entertainment was over. Well, it began like entertainment but it finished rather differently and they are glad to escape. There was no sense that this was a job well done, a good day's work. All of a sudden they realized what had happened; they woke up to the facts. Just a few days ago the crowd had been so happy to see Jesus arrive. The people had been singing and dancing round in the street, gathering to hear every word that he had to say, glad that he was challenging so much and so many people. Then the mood had changed and they had been caught up in that. Now, as they slouched off, it felt as if they had been used, manipulated, as though they too had been pawns in a bigger game.

They remembered what they had shouted just a few hours before:

'His blood be on us and on our children!'
(Matthew 27.25)

What had they been saying? What madness had come upon them?

What madness comes upon us when we are used by others, when we agree to something we would never really agree to? What madness comes upon us when we nod a wrong decision through, when we acquiesce to something – well, just for the sake of it? What madness comes upon us when we allow a racist, a sexist, a homophobic comment to pass without challenge? What madness comes upon us when we cry with the crowd, 'His blood be on us and on our children' and then we look at our children?

> Jesus, Lamb of God, have mercy on us.
> Jesus, bearer of our sins, have mercy on us.
> Jesus, redeemer of the world, grant us peace.[17]

4.00pm

Blood and water

Since it was the day of Preparation, the Jews did not want the bodies left on the cross during the sabbath, especially because that sabbath was a day of great solemnity. So they asked Pilate to have the legs of the crucified men broken and the bodies removed. Then the soldiers came and broke the legs of the first and of the other who had been crucified with him. But when they came to Jesus and saw that he was already dead, they did not break his legs. Instead, one of the soldiers pierced his side with a spear, and at once blood and water came out. (He who saw this has testified so that you also may believe. His testimony is true, and he knows that he tells the truth.) These things occurred so that the scripture might be fulfilled, 'None of his bones shall be broken.' And again another passage of scripture says, 'They will look on the one whom they have pierced.' (John 19.31–37)

So the other two men were still alive after Jesus had died. The clock had kept on ticking for them and the agony had continued. The repentant thief saw Jesus die and knew that he was making a welcome ready for him in his king-dom. But too much time had been wasted already on this, and the Sabbath was approaching.

So the soldiers come along and break the legs of those who are still alive. Crucifixion kills in the end through asphyxi-ation. The one crucified no longer has the strength to haul their body up to take a breath. While the body hangs from the arms the chest is crushed and you cannot breathe. So if you break the legs then the person crucified can no longer raise themselves up and so they quickly choke and die.

But Jesus was dead already. So just to make sure they push a spear, a lance, into his side and out flows blood and water. Might this be a sacramental sign to us? There are two Dominical Sacraments as they are called – sacraments ordained by the Lord – baptism and the Eucharist. Perhaps John, in his Gospel, is pointing us to these sacraments flowing from the side of Christ.

Or perhaps it is a reminder to us that in the person of Christ we find humanity and divinity perfectly balanced, in perfect harmony. Jesus is fully human and fully God and out of his one side blood and water flow. It reminds me of the prayer that the priest says as water and wine are mixed in the chalice at the Eucharist.

> By the mystery of this water and wine
> may we come to share in the divinity of Christ
> who humbled himself to share in our humanity.

6.00pm

The longest day

When it was evening, there came a rich man from Arimathea, named Joseph, who was also a disciple of Jesus. He went to Pilate and asked for the body of Jesus; then Pilate ordered it to be given to him. So Joseph took the body and wrapped it in a clean linen cloth and laid it in his own new tomb, which he had hewn in the rock. He then rolled a great stone to the door of the tomb and went away. Mary Magdalene and the other Mary were there, sitting opposite the tomb. (Matthew 27.57–61)

It has been a long day, the longest the world has known. Now they have placed the body of Jesus, the lifeless body of Jesus, in the tomb that has been given to them by a stranger, Joseph of Arimathea. But what choice do the disciples have? They have no choice; either this stranger's tomb or the body is taken away and thrown in a common grave, in a pit. So they accept the gift and, carefully and lovingly, they carry the body of their friend, their Master, their Teacher, their Lord, from the barren hillside into a garden where the tomb has been created. And in the

gathering gloom they lay the shrouded body there, roll
the stone in place and, embracing the women, who are
watching, leave.

> Lord Jesus Christ, Son of the living God,
> who at this evening hour lay in the tomb
> and so hallowed the grave
> to be a bed of hope for all who put their trust in you:
> give us such sorrow for our sins,
> which were the cause of your passion,
> that when our bodies lie in the dust,
> our souls may live with you for ever.
> Amen.[18]

Holy Saturday

9.00am

They rested

On the sabbath they rested according to the command-ment. (Luke 23.56)

And we too rest and wait to see what tomorrow brings.

> In the depths of our isolation
> we cry to you, Lord God:
> give light in our darkness
> and bring us out of the prison of our despair;
> through Jesus Christ our Lord.
> Amen.

12.00 noon

While we rest

For Christ also suffered for sins once for all, the righteous for the unrighteous, in order to bring you to God. He was put to death in the flesh, but made alive in the spirit, in which also he went and made a proclamation to the spirits in prison, who in former times did not obey, when God waited patiently in the days of Noah, during the building of the ark, in which a few, that is, eight people, were saved through water. (1 Peter 3.18–20)

The disciples were forced to rest and to wait. But was Jesus resting? St Peter in his First Letter suggests otherwise, as does the tradition for this Holy Saturday. In the Apostles' Creed we say that he 'descended into hell', and it must have been on this day that all this happened. Like a super-hero, Jesus enters the place of our greatest fears, that prison in which humankind had been kept, from which there was no escape and brings those lost in death to life. This is called 'the harrowing of hell'. It's an interesting word that we use. To harrow is an agricultural term and it refers to the process of breaking up the soil. Christ breaks into hell and, in the tradition, finds our first parents Adam and Eve, and the righteous souls from the Old Testament and brings them out into the new life that his death has secured for us.

I remember going for the first time to the church of St Saviour in Chora in Istanbul. There in a separate chapel to what would have been the main church is a perfectly preserved fresco in the apse where the altar would have stood, of the harrowing of hell. In it Christ is literally pulling Adam and Eve out of shattered hell and into new life. He has each by a wrist, he isn't leading them, he is literally pulling them out, this rescue of those who perhaps do not want to be rescued, reluctant to leave the prison they have known, fearful of what lies beyond. It is the most amazing, vigorous, energetic image.

But I think that the fresco reveals a truth about ourselves. We can easily find ourselves resisting God; it seems easier to be where we are than where God wants us to be, in the dark, rather than the light, in the prison of our making rather than enjoying the freedom in Christ which is all gift. We can be perverse beings, and Jesus in hell challenges this tendency and proclaims new life to the spirits in prison.

This was no day of rest for Jesus – the work of resurrection had begun. But we, with the disciples, must wait.

> Lord, challenge my perversity,
> challenge my complacency,
> and in the vigour of your new life
> draw me into light and freedom.
> Amen.

Easter Day

6.00am

Easter in real time

Early on the first day of the week, while it was still dark, Mary Magdalene came to the tomb and saw that the stone had been removed from the tomb. So she ran and went to Simon Peter and the other disciple, the one whom Jesus loved, and said to them, 'They have taken the Lord out of the tomb, and we do not know where they have laid him.' Then Peter and the other disciple set out and went towards the tomb. The two were running together, but the other disciple outran Peter and reached the tomb first. He bent down to look in and saw the linen wrappings lying there, but he did not go in. Then Simon Peter came, following him, and went into the tomb. He saw the linen wrappings lying there, and the cloth that had been on Jesus' head, not lying with the linen wrappings but rolled up in a place by itself. Then the other disciple, who reached the tomb first, also went in, and he saw and believed; for as yet they did not understand the scripture, that he must rise from the dead. Then the disciples returned to their homes. (John 20.1–10)

It had been a long Saturday. It was meant to be a day of rest, but how could she rest? She wanted to be with him, at the tomb, in that garden, able to complete what had been begun, able to care for him as he had cared for her. So, when the first streaks of dawn coloured the Jerusalem sky she left the house and made for the garden.

The air was fresh and clean; it was a new day, but as beautiful as it was the heaviness hung over her. She couldn't escape what she had seen. The one who had given her back her life, the one who recognized the person she was, who had saved her from herself, the one she had followed and ministered to, the one she had anointed and washed with her own tears, she saw him die. His life ebbed away and so did hers. He died and she felt as though she died with him.

It was still the half-light of dawn when she arrived but she could see immediately that all was not right. The stone that had sealed the tomb was rolled away. She was petrified and, without waiting, ran back for Peter and John. She needed them now. She had wanted to be on her own, but now she needed them to help her, to look into the tomb and see what was going on.

So together they ran back to the tomb. John was so much younger than Peter and that showed in the race to the garden. He got there first but his youth, which had given him the energy, kept him back from going in. It was Peter, headstrong, impetuous, fearless, who went in and discovered the truth – Jesus was not there, just the cloths in which they had bound him, just the shroud in which they had buried him, just the cloth that had covered his face. And all was neat and orderly. This was no grave robbery in which everything was in disarray. All the cloths had been folded – and Jesus was gone.

SLEEP, sleep, old Sun! thou canst not have repast
As yet the wound thou took'st on Friday last;
Sleep then and rest; the world may bear thy stay,
A better sun rose before thee to-day.

This is the beginning of a poem by John Donne called 'Easter Day'. He speaks to the sun. It is not needed this day. The son has risen; it is a different dawn, a different colour that streaks the sky, the colour of resurrection. But at the moment, Mary and the disciples do not know this. Instead, grief has added to their grief and Mary stays at the tomb weeping.

Risen Lord,
make yourself known,
stay in the shadows no longer,
meet us with
resurrection life.
Amen.

7.00am

Called by name

But Mary stood weeping outside the tomb. As she wept, she bent over to look into the tomb; and she saw two angels in white, sitting where the body of Jesus had been lying, one at the head and the other at the feet. They said to her, 'Woman, why are you weeping?' She said to them, 'They have taken away my Lord, and I do not know where they have laid him.' When she had said this, she turned round and saw Jesus standing there, but she did not know that it was Jesus. Jesus said to her, 'Woman, why are you weeping? For whom are you looking?' Supposing him to be the gardener, she said to him, 'Sir, if you have carried him away, tell me where you have laid him, and I will take him away.' Jesus said to her, 'Mary!' She turned and said to him in Hebrew, 'Rabbouni!' (which means Teacher). Jesus said to her, 'Do not hold on to me, because I have not yet ascended to the Father. But go to my brothers and say to them, "I am ascending to my Father and your Father, to my God and your God."' Mary Magdalene went and announced

to the disciples, 'I have seen the Lord'; and she told them
that he had said these things to her. (John 20.11–18)

The day was still beginning but for Mary time had
stopped. The others had left her and she was there outside
the tomb. The grass was dew-jewelled and she got up from
where she had been kneeling, she went to look inside the
tomb, to see what Peter and John had seen. She expected
it empty as they had said, but it wasn't. There were two
people there; well, they looked like people, but in white;
calm, beautiful, full of messages it seemed. She had no
fear. They saw her tears and with voices like the gentle
breeze of dawn asked her why she was weeping and she
told them.

She felt as though she were no longer alone in another way.
It is strange how we can sense when someone is behind us,
and that was what happened. Mary turned from these two
beautiful creatures and looked back into the garden. She
was looking from the darkness of the tomb into what was
the first light of the new day and there was someone there.

Was it her eyes not coping with the shift from dark to
light; was it the tears filming her eyes, obscuring her sight;
was it the quality of this first light? Whatever, she couldn't
make out who it was.

He asked her the same question that she had been asked in
the tomb: 'Why are you weeping?' And then, 'For whom
are you looking?'

Who was this person? She couldn't see; she couldn't think;
all she knew was that she wanted Jesus and to be out of
this strange disturbing, yet peaceful place. She thought

this stranger must work in the garden – at least he might know what had happened.

She was looking back now into the tomb as he spoke to her, and she said, 'Sir, if you have carried him away, tell me where you have laid him, and I will take him away.' She was looking where the body had been, she was looking at the cloths lying folded, she was looking at the emptiness within, which was like the emptiness in her heart, and then life changed.

In the famous 'poem' by Henry Scott Holland, so loved at funerals, 'Death is Nothing at All', there are these lines:

> *Call me by my old familiar name.*
> *Speak to me in the easy way*
> *which you always used.*
> *Put no difference into your tone.*
> *Wear no forced air of solemnity or sorrow.*[19]

It is when Mary hears her name in the garden, in the dawn, at the tomb, through her grief, that resurrection and truth and life break through and she wakes up to a new reality, *the* new reality. Only her name could break the seal.

As the prophet Isaiah says

> *But now thus says the LORD,*
> *he who created you, O Jacob,*
> *he who formed you, O Israel:*
> *Do not fear, for I have redeemed you;*
> *I have called you by name, you are mine.*
> *When you pass through the waters, I will be with you;*
> *and through the rivers, they shall not overwhelm you;*

when you walk through fire you shall not be burned,
and the flame shall not consume you.
(Isaiah 43.1–2)

'I have called you by name.' We are known by God for
who we are, personally, intimately. Jesus knew the real
Mary, not the notorious sinner from Magdala but the
beloved of God, created in God's image, loved by God.
Jesus had died for her as he died for you, and he called her
into life by name, just as he called Lazarus back to life, by
name. And he calls us back to life, by name.

> Lord God,
> at my baptism I was named as your child.
> Call me into your new life;
> may I hear your voice
> and recognize my new self
> in you.
> Amen.

12 noon

On the road

Now on that same day two of them were going to a village called Emmaus, about seven miles from Jerusalem, and talking with each other about all these things that had happened. While they were talking and discussing, Jesus himself came near and went with them, but their eyes were kept from recognizing him. And he said to them, 'What are you discussing with each other while you walk along?' They stood still, looking sad. Then one of them, whose name was Cleopas, answered him, 'Are you the only stranger in Jerusalem who does not know the things that have taken place there in these days?' He asked them, 'What things?' They replied, 'The things about Jesus of Nazareth, who was a prophet mighty in deed and word before God and all the people, and how our chief priests and leaders handed him over to be condemned to death and crucified him. But we had hoped that he was the one to redeem Israel. Yes, and besides all this, it is now the third day since these things took place. Moreover, some women of our group astounded us. They were at the tomb early this morning, and when

they did not find his body there, they came back and told
us that they had indeed seen a vision of angels who said
that he was alive. Some of those who were with us went
to the tomb and found it just as the women had said;
but they did not see him.' Then he said to them, 'Oh,
how foolish you are, and how slow of heart to believe
all that the prophets have declared! Was it not necessary
that the Messiah should suffer these things and then
enter into his glory?' Then beginning with Moses and
all the prophets, he interpreted to them the things about
himself in all the scriptures. (Luke 24.13–27)

Jerusalem was beginning to empty. The festival was over
and it was time to get back home and pick up the pieces
of normal life again. People had come from all over the
country and from all the places where the Jewish community was living. Simon had come from Cyrene, others
from other parts of the Diaspora. For some it had simply
been a good Passover at the heart of their nation, at the
heart of their faith. For others it had been life-changing.

Simon had been called from the crowd to carry a prisoner's
cross. His life was changed for ever. Where would he go,
what would he do? Just going back to normal seemed
ridiculous. Others had joined a procession into the city a
week ago, following a band of disciples with their teacher;
then they had seen that man again, on trial before the
governor. They had followed a grisly procession outside
the city wall and watched the man die. They wouldn't
forget it.

Others had been more intimately involved. Cleopas was
heading out of town with the crowds, heading back to his
home in Emmaus and he was travelling with – well, we

don't know who it was. I always imagine though that it was with his wife, Mary. In St John's Gospel we are told that beneath the cross of Jesus stood his mother Mary, Mary Magdalene and Mary 'the wife of Clopas' (John 19.25). Is this another way of spelling Cleopas? It most probably is. And John tells us that this woman was 'his mother's sister'. We don't know whether she was actually Mary's sister, Mary – it would seem unlikely to have two girls named the same – or her sister-in-law, therefore Joseph's sister Mary.

Whatever the relationship is in these precise terms, it would seem that these two disciples are the aunt and uncle of Jesus, family members who were on the edge of the group of disciples but who had been sharing the Passover with other members of the family in Jerusalem. Luke tells us that Mary and Joseph came to Jerusalem for the Passover each year (Luke 2.41) and so they probably shared in that with the wider family – just as we meet up with the wider family for Christmas, visit the aunts and uncles.

So Cleopas and Mary are heading out of town. Perhaps they can't wait to leave the city. Seeing Jesus die was heart-rending; they were grief-stricken and exhausted, supporting Mary in her agony. And as they left, rumours were beginning to circulate among their friends that Jesus had been seen alive. They couldn't believe it. So they headed home, home where they could get back to normal – but it would be a new normality.

And like any couple, they talked and talked, sharing memories, sharing thoughts. So much to think about. There were a great many people on the road, so when someone caught them up it didn't seem strange. But what was strange was that someone heading in the same direction knew nothing of what had been happening in Jerusalem.

'How could this man not know?' they thought. But they filled him in with the details, shared with him their experience.

And then he speaks.

The account of the experience on the road to Emmaus is, for me, one of the most important gospel passages. It is about the Christian life, it is about the Eucharist, it is about knowing God, knowing Jesus.

In his book *With Burning Hearts*, Henri Nouwen says of the Emmaus story:

> *As the story speaks of loss, presence, invitation, communion, and mission it embraces the five main aspects of the Eucharistic celebration. Together they form a movement, the movement from resentment to gratitude, that is, from a hardened heart to a grateful heart.*[20]

It is this movement that we are caught up in as we too travel with Cleopas and Mary and with the stranger who seems to know so little but knows so much.

Walk with us, Lord,
on our journey
and open the scriptures to us.
Amen.

5.00pm

At the table

> *As they came near the village to which they were going,*
> *he walked ahead as if he were going on. But they urged*
> *him strongly, saying, 'Stay with us, because it is almost*
> *evening and the day is now nearly over.' So he went in*
> *to stay with them. When he was at the table with them,*
> *he took bread, blessed and broke it, and gave it to them.*
> *Then their eyes were opened, and they recognized him;*
> *and he vanished from their sight. They said to each*
> *other, 'Were not our hearts burning within us while he*
> *was talking to us on the road, while he was opening the*
> *scriptures to us?' (Luke 24.28–32)*

It was a seven-mile walk from Jerusalem to Emmaus and
they had been talking all the time. The stranger was still
with them, and he was fascinating. The time had flown
past and now the three of them were alone on the road;
people had gone off to different villages, some to inns to
spend the night, but Emmaus was not far and as the sun
began to sink behind the hills they arrived at the edge of
the village.

It was a famous place. This was where the Ark of the Covenant had rested at the house of Abinadab, the place where the prophet Jeremiah had been born. The village had been there for a long time – people knew it as 'Grape Village' because of the wonderful vines and the good wine that was produced there. It was a lovely place, it was home.

They arrived at their house but the stranger continued walking. 'Stay with us,' said Mary and Cleopas, 'it is almost evening and the day is now nearly over. We have bread and the wine is very good.'

So the stranger came in and the table was quickly set and they took their seats. Where the Ark of God, the very presence of God had rested, the stranger took his seat. And then the strangest thing happened. The stranger became the host – not in a rude way, not in an inappropriate way, it seemed so natural, so right. He took the bread and, instead of Clepoas doing this, he said the blessing, broke and shared the bread – and they knew who he was.

He was gone.

As quickly as they recognized him, he was gone.

I said that this Gospel is about the Eucharist. Whenever we celebrate the sacrament we begin by reading the word, by reading the scriptures. They are broken open for us. Then we move to the table and bread is taken and broken for us. We share the word, broken open for us; we share the bread, broken for us, and in his word and in his bread we recognize Jesus in the midst.

Cleopas and Mary described their hearts 'burning within them'. The spirit of Jesus was upon them, within them, like the early flames of Pentecost, setting them on fire, with presence, with love. The spirit of God had entered their hearts; the spirit of Jesus was filling their lives. Their eyes, their minds, their hearts, their lives had been opened to the living Lord, the living God.

> Risen Christ,
> for whom no door is locked, no entrance barred:
> open the doors of our hearts,
> that we may seek the good of others
> and walk the joyful road of sacrifice and peace,
> to the praise of God the Father.
> Amen.[21]

6.00pm

The Lord has risen indeed

That same hour they got up and returned to Jerusalem; and they found the eleven and their companions gathered together. They were saying, 'The Lord has risen indeed, and he has appeared to Simon!' Then they told what had happened on the road, and how he had been made known to them in the breaking of the bread.
(Luke 24.33–35)

It might be late, it might be dark, it might be seven miles back, they might be tired and the meal might still be on the table – but nothing would stop them. They grabbed their cloaks and headed back the way they had come. They were on fire with the Spirit. They had to tell the others. This was such good news; they could barely hold it in. And the miles flew past. What had seemed a long journey before seemed no distance now, as though they were whisked along by God.

They got to the place where the disciples were staying with Mary. The doors were locked – they must all be in fear.

But they banged on the door, insistent, and eventually it was opened to them. They burst into the room. But instead of a room filled with grief, people were aglow with joy.

They couldn't get their news out before one of the others said, 'The Lord has risen indeed, and he has appeared to Simon!' They could have been disappointed. They wanted to share their good news, but they were filled with joy and then they told everyone about what had happened to them on the journey and how they knew him 'in the breaking of the bread'.

On most occasions when we celebrate the Eucharist we invite people to communion with these words:

> *Jesus is the Lamb of God*
> *who takes away the sin of the world.*
> *Blessed are those who are called to his supper.*
>
> **Lord, I am not worthy to receive you,**
> **but only say the word, and I shall be healed.**[22]

It is a moment to look up and see the priest holding the host, the bread, before us and to recognize the presence, the real presence, of Jesus with us. Every time we come to the altar it is an Emmaus moment, we know the Lord 'in the breaking of the bread'. It is a resurrection moment, for the Lord is risen and is with us. It is a moment of Good News, and that news is being proclaimed ahead of us and our lives and our experience of Jesus can confirm what others have said. We are all part of this 'movement to … a grateful heart' as Nouwen describes it. As the hymn puts it:

EASTER DAY

We have a gospel to proclaim
Good news for all in all the earth;
The gospel of a Saviour's name:
We sing His glory, tell His worth.[23]

Living God,
your Son made himself known to his disciples
in the breaking of bread:
open the eyes of our faith,
that we may see him in all his redeeming work;
who is alive and reigns, now and for ever.
Amen.[24]

7.00pm

Easter breaks out

When it was evening on that day, the first day of the week, and the doors of the house where the disciples had met were locked for fear of the Jews, Jesus came and stood among them and said, 'Peace be with you.' After he said this, he showed them his hands and his side. Then the disciples rejoiced when they saw the Lord. Jesus said to them again, 'Peace be with you. As the Father has sent me, so I send you.' When he had said this, he breathed on them and said to them, 'Receive the Holy Spirit. If you forgive the sins of any, they are forgiven them; if you retain the sins of any, they are retained.' (John 20.19–23)

John tells another story of that first day of resurrection. There is so much in the gospel accounts and not everything fits into a clean, clear narrative. As we have followed the events of this week in 'real time' I have had to do some creative juggling with the gospel accounts to make them fit. As I said at the outset, I hope the biblical purists forgive me!

But this is another of those critical encounters with the risen Lord. When Cleopas and his wife arrive back at the room where the disciples are, in St Luke's Gospel, those there are full of joy at the news that Peter has seen the Lord. In John's Gospel it is evening but the disciples are locked away for fear. And then into their locked space Jesus breaks in and says, 'Peace be with you', and to prove it he shows them his wounds, his hands and his side.

The disciples are filled with joy and, recognizing the Lord, recognizing the truth of the resurrection, they are commissioned for ministry.

Priests share in Christ's priesthood. This is not to diminish in any way the ministry of the whole people of God, the ministry of the laity. Through our baptism we are all called into ministry, we each receive a vocation. But from the first the church has set aside some to work for the whole church and to represent to the whole body that priestly ministry in which we all share. Priesthood is Christ's priesthood, held by the church, the people of God, and exercised by some on behalf of the whole.

Jesus breathes on the disciples, as with the breath of the Holy Spirit at Pentecost, and sends them, filled with that Holy Spirit, to witness and to forgive. It is that ministry of reconciliation that is such an important priestly ministry that it has become part of the definition of what makes us priests. In the Ordination Service for Priests in the Book of Common Prayer this is made explicit.

RECEIVE the Holy Ghost for the office and work of a Priest in the Church of God, now committed unto thee by the imposition of our hands. Whose sins thou dost

forgive, they are forgiven; and whose sins thou dost re-
tain, they are retained. And be thou a faithful dispenser
of the Word of God, and of his holy Sacraments; In the
Name of the Father, and of the Son, and of the Holy
Ghost. Amen.

In the Upper Room, on the day of resurrection, the church's ministry is formed. The risen Christ forms us as a eucharistic, reconciling, peace-filled community, alive in the Spirit and in his resurrection. Is this the church we truly are? Do we bring peace, do we bring reconciliation, do we witness effectively to the reality of God, the reality of Christ? I love the church, but I love Christ more, and where we fail Christ as his church then we need to look again at our life in the light of resurrection. The good news we have to proclaim is 'Peace be with you!'

And that should be good news for every person, in every place, at every time, in real time. If that is not the message that people hear us proclaiming then we are not the people of the Upper Room, of the empty tomb, then we are not the Easter people of God, the children of the resurrection.

> God of glory,
> by the raising of your Son
> you have broken the chains of death and hell:
> fill your Church with faith and hope;
> for a new day has dawned
> and the way to life stands open
> in our Saviour Jesus Christ.
> Amen.[25]

Easter Monday

The doubter

But Thomas (who was called the Twin), one of the twelve, was not with them when Jesus came. So the other disciples told him, 'We have seen the Lord.' But he said to them, 'Unless I see the mark of the nails in his hands, and put my finger in the mark of the nails and my hand in his side, I will not believe.' (John 20.24–25)

Thomas came back into the room. When he'd left, to go off to do what he had to do (we don't know what that was), they were all despondent. He was glad to get out of the intensity of the space and to be able to walk a bit and clear his head. He was a practical kind of guy – he liked things clear. Some weeks ago Jesus had been speaking about going and preparing a place for them and that they were to follow. He'd shouted out from the sidelines:

'Lord, we do not know where you are going. How can we know the way?' (John 14.5)

The others had laughed – but it was true. Unless they knew where he was off to, how could they follow him? He wasn't trying to be funny – but to be honest the others sometimes had their heads in the clouds. And the answer from Jesus, which came immediately, sounded great, but, well, it was hardly a set of coordinates!

Jesus said to him, 'I am the way, and the truth, and the life. No one comes to the Father except through me.' (John 14.6)

But there was no doubt about his commitment. As Thomas walked, keeping in the shadows so that no one spotted him as one of the 'out-of-town' followers of Jesus, he remembered when they were heading to Bethany because they had the news that their friend Lazarus had died. When Jesus said that they were going to see Mary and Martha, Lazarus' sisters, for some reason he'd again shouted from the edge:

'Let us also go, that we may die with him.' (John 11.16)

It seems ironic now that Jesus was dead and he was still alive.

But when they let him back into the locked room, they all descended on him, not to find out where he had been and for so long, but to tell him that Jesus was not dead, he was alive and he had been with them in that room. Their faces were beaming. They were mad, thought Thomas; they should get some fresh air – once more, heads in the clouds.

And when he said to them,

'Unless I see the mark of the nails in his hands, and put my finger in the mark of the nails and my hand in his side, I will not believe'

they looked crestfallen. But why should he just believe their words? He was a man who needed evidence, he wanted a map to know where they were going, he had his feet on the ground, not his head in the clouds and they knew that and they'd have to accept it. Unless he had the evidence in his hands he was not going to believe, however many times they told him – and they did, time after time – that Jesus had been with them. He wanted, he needed, to see for himself.

We talk a great deal about mission and evangelism in the church, and that is right. But it can make me feel a bit guilty. How do I convince the sceptical, how do I convert the uninterested, how do I change the cynical, so that they believe in Jesus as I do? 'Show me ... prove it to me ... where's the evidence.' What can I show them, how can I prove it, what evidence have I got? If the disciples in the Upper Room couldn't convince their friend about the resurrection when he had been with them all the time, when he had seen Lazarus walk from the tomb, when he'd seen the son of the widow of Nain come down from his bier, when he had seen Jairus' daughter brought back to life, then what chance have I got?

St Francis of Assisi is always quoted as saying something like, 'Preach the gospel at all times; use words if you must.' When people met Francis they knew they met Jesus. He bore on his body the marks of Jesus. It may not be quite like that for us, but the only way we can witness to, prove, explain, convince, is by people meeting Jesus in us and by showing that for us he is 'the way, and the truth, and the life', that those are our coordinates for our lives. Our lives have to be an eloquent sermon, a living word for the living God.

Eternal God,
whose Son Jesus Christ is the way, the truth, and
   the life:
grant us to walk in his way,
to rejoice in his truth,
and to share his risen life;
who is alive and reigns, now and for ever.
Amen.[26]

Easter 1

7.00pm

My Lord and my God

> *A week later his disciples were again in the house, and Thomas was with them. Although the doors were shut, Jesus came and stood among them and said, 'Peace be with you.' Then he said to Thomas, 'Put your finger here and see my hands. Reach out your hand and put it in my side. Do not doubt but believe.' Thomas answered him, 'My Lord and my God!' Jesus said to him, 'Have you believed because you have seen me? Blessed are those who have not seen and yet have come to believe.' (John 20.26–29)*

A whole week had passed; a week in which they could come to terms with what had happened to them, what had happened to Jesus. For most people life had moved on, but not for them. They were still behind closed doors, still living in fear of facing death as Jesus had. So they kept together in the place where they felt safe and with the people with whom they felt safe.

A whole week had passed in which they had been trying to convince Thomas about what they had seen, what they had experienced in that room. But it didn't matter who told him, or how forcefully they tried, it made no difference. He kept coming back with the same phrase:

'Unless I see the mark of the nails in his hands, and put my finger in the mark of the nails and my hand in his side, I will not believe.'

'I will not believe' – it was like a nail in the hands, like a spear in the side. For him to say that to them, for him not to believe them, ignoring the testimony of his ten friends. But he stayed with them and they stayed with him.

And now it was a week since the message had come to this room from the women that the tomb was empty, since Peter arrived back to tell them it was true, since Cleopas and his wife had hurried back to tell them of their experience on the road, since Jesus stood among them and showed them his hands and his side. And Thomas was with them – and so was Jesus. Just as before, all of a sudden he was there, and with the same greeting, 'Peace be with you.'

Jesus immediately turned to Thomas, who was amazed.

'Put your finger here and see my hands. Reach out your hand and put it in my side. Do not doubt but believe.'

We are not told that Thomas actually did this. The invitation was made but would Thomas really have done that – or was seeing sufficient? He had said:

'Unless I see the mark of the nails in his hands, and put my finger in the mark of the nails and my hand in his side, I will not believe.'

But when push came to shove, did he really need to do this?

Instead, what we get is the most beautiful profession of faith as Thomas simply says

'My Lord and my God.'

The great Baptist preacher Charles Spurgeon said in a sermon delivered at the Metropolitan Tabernacle at the Elephant and Castle in 1884:

Thomas cries in ecstasy, 'My Lord and my God!' He is amazed at the discovery which he has made and probably, also, at the fact that he has not seen it long before. Why, he might have known it and ought to have perceived it years before! Had he not been present when Jesus trod the sea? When He hushed the winds and bade the waters sleep? Had he not seen Him open the blind eyes and unstop the deaf ears? Why did he not cry, 'My Lord and my God', then? Thomas had been slow to learn and the Lord might have said to him, as He did to Philip, 'Have I been so long time with you, and yet have you not known Me?' Now, all of a sudden, he does know his Lord – knows Him to such a surprising extent that such knowledge is too wonderful for him!

Spurgeon is right. This is an ecstatic utterance and Jesus does not deny it. Thomas has expressed the truth that so many find it hard to believe, that Jesus is both Lord and God, our Lord and God.

This declaration of faith I was taught to say as the host is lifted before us in the Eucharist. As the priest invites us to communion – 'Jesus is the Lamb of God ...', 'Draw near with faith ...' – in our hearts we should be saying with Thomas: 'My Lord and my God!' It is the perfect way to approach Jesus who approaches us in the Mass and gives himself fully to us as he offered himself fully to Thomas.

It is true that we do not have what Thomas was given, the joy of seeing the Lord in that way. But there is a sting in the tail for Thomas. Yes, he has come out with the shortest, neatest confessional statement, but he needed the evidence to do this. But Jesus calls us 'blessed' because we believe without seeing – and that, as Jesus acknowledges, is much more difficult. There is no dishonour in doubting, no disgrace in questioning, no shame in challenging the things that we are taught as Christians. But when the questions have been asked we need to have the confidence to stand before Jesus and say with Thomas, 'My Lord and my God', and we can only do that when fear has been cast out by love. Fear is the true opposite of doubt and often holds us back from believing, but the love of God casts out our fear and leads us to deeper faith.

> Jesus,
> when it is fear that stops me believing
> cast it out with the love
> I see on the cross
> and in the empty tomb
> and give me the confidence to say,
> 'My Lord and my God'.
> Amen.

Easter 2

The story continues

Now Jesus did many other signs in the presence of his disciples, which are not written in this book. But these are written so that you may come to believe that Jesus is the Messiah, the Son of God, and that through believing you may have life in his name. (John 20.30–31)

Harry Potter ran to seven books but J. K. Rowling had already been outdone by Enid Blyton who managed twenty-one Famous Five novels. I'm sure there is always more that a novelist can write and we have seen some intriguing sequels written in modern times to classics by those who thought they could complete an unfinished task – *Gone with the Wind*, *Pride and Prejudice*, even *Winnie the Pooh* have all been given the sequel treatment. Because we want to know what else happened. On many occasions I've closed a book and wished it could have gone on – 'But what happened next?' I've asked myself.

St John intrigues us by telling us that so many things happened 'which are not written in this book'. And we want to know – what things? Tell us more. John concludes his Gospel in this way:

There are also many other things that Jesus did; if every one of them were written down, I suppose that the world itself could not contain the books that would be written.
(John 21.25)

Even more hints of how much could be said. Of course there is more in the post-resurrection accounts in the Gospels than I have mentioned. I thought I should end somewhere but the temptation is to mention more and more. The wonderful encounter by the Sea of Galilee, the third appearance of Jesus after the resurrection, (John 21.9–14), and what is known as 'Peter's Primacy', which follows immediately on (John 21.15–24), are a case in point. Luke mentions an appearance in the Upper Room following the arrival back of the travellers to Emmaus (Luke 24.36–49) and ends with the ascension (Luke 24.50–53).

St Mark's Gospel ends in a rather peculiar way. In bibles you will find that the Gospel ends at Mark 16.8 with the disciples fleeing the tomb, 'for they were afraid'. Then you may find two other endings – the shorter and the longer. It would seem that the original ending was too abrupt for the early church and so people, helpfully, and I'm sure, inspired by God, added the various endings. This is not to deny that they are part of the canon of scripture but it is interesting in that we want more.

Matthew's Gospel includes just one appearance, an attempt to further discredit the Jewish authorities (Matthew 28.11–15), and then an account of the ascension.

Of course, in the early church there were a great many attempts to get more books in the series and to write some sequels. The Gnostic Gospels, as they are called, are a series of 51 documents written from the second to the fourth centuries and disputed by the church, so not included in the final canon of scripture, which was settled and agreed probably around 393.

What John is clear about, though, is that what is written is there to lead us into faith, into belief in Jesus, Messiah, Son of God, and that this belief will lead us into life, eternal life. The truth is that the story of Jesus is still being written in your life and mine, on the pages of your life and mine. The story is never complete, the risen Lord is always present, and as the Lord says in the book of Deuteronomy:

You shall put these words of mine in your heart and soul.
(Deuteronomy 11.18)

Lord,
write your Good News in my life
that I may be a living gospel
as you are my living Lord
and that your story may be told
in the lives of all your people.
Amen.

Ascension Day

8.00am

Time has passed

Then Jesus led them out as far as Bethany, and, lifting up his hands, he blessed them. While he was blessing them, he withdrew from them and was carried up into heaven. And they worshipped him, and returned to Jerusalem with great joy; and they were continually in the temple blessing God. (Luke 24.50–53)

It's forty days since the resurrection of Jesus happened. The clock has still been ticking; we are still in real time. We have all gone back to our daily lives, our jobs, the demands of family and friends, the things that keep us busy, the ways in which we spend our time. Time has passed. And time has passed for the disciples – but we are not given any clues about how it has been passed.

To be honest, the forty days is a traditional timing for the ascension and isn't mentioned in scripture. It may have been established in relation to Pentecost, which is of course a 'real time' event in that we can accurately say when it occurred in relation to the events of Easter. But for this purpose we will stay with the tradition.

This still leaves us with the intriguing question of what was going on for those forty days. It would certainly seem that the disciples were still in Jerusalem, for it is from the city that they go out to the Mount of the Ascension, which Luke tells us, in the Gospel, was near Bethany. In the Acts of the Apostles (also ascribed to Luke) it says, after the event, that they 'returned to Jerusalem from the mount called Olivet'. So the Mount of Olives is as good a place to remember this event as anywhere else.

The traditional site visited by pilgrims is on the summit of the Mount of Olives, the place from which the palm procession begins. So the triumph of the entry into Jerusalem and the triumph of the ascension, the entry into heaven, are linked in a wonderful way.

Before the conversion of Constantine in AD 312, early Christians remembered the ascension of Jesus in a cave on the Mount of Olives. By 384, the place of the ascension was venerated on the present site, up the hill from the cave in a church first built in 390. The Chapel of the Ascension that pilgrims visit today is a Christian and Muslim holy site. As an added bonus, in the small octagonal church/mosque is a stone imprinted with what some claim to be the footprint of Jesus.

Whatever the historical accuracy may be, the ascension marks a moment of transition for the disciples and the beginning of a time of expectant waiting. We imagine that for forty days they have experienced the presence of the risen Christ with them in a particular way; after all, Luke says 'while staying with them' (Acts 1.4). Jesus has been staying with them, now he is leaving them, now there is a change. It's intriguing to think that we have only been given a taste of the experience of the risen Jesus that they experienced in all its fullness, for this long period of time.

But the truth is that we too have been experiencing the reality of the risen Jesus in the reality of our lives during these forty days. A few years ago I went to Zimbabwe to visit the diocese of Masvingo, with which Southwark Cathedral is linked. One of the lasting impressions I have is of the joy and vibrancy of the worship in which I shared – worship full of the reality of God, full of the life that we experience when we know Jesus. That is true wherever we are, and the presence of the Paschal Candle, burning in our churches throughout these days, is a constant and living reminder of the constant and living presence of Jesus with us. However these days have passed for you, the Lord has been present with you, in your real time.

> Ever present, risen Lord,
> may I never forget that you are with me,
> wherever I go,
> whatever I do,
> for forty days,
> for always.
> Amen.

12.00 noon

Stay

> *They returned to Jerusalem from the mount called*
> *Olivet, which is near Jerusalem, a Sabbath day's journey*
> *away. When they had entered the city, they went to*
> *the room upstairs where they were staying, Peter, and*
> *John, and James, and Andrew, Philip and Thomas,*
> *Bartholomew and Matthew, James son of Alphaeus, and*
> *Simon the Zealot, and Judas son of James. All these were*
> *constantly devoting themselves to prayer, together with*
> *certain women, including Mary the mother of Jesus, as*
> *well as his brothers.* (Acts 1.12–14)

Luke tells us that they were looking up into heaven as
Jesus was taken from them and then two angels are standing there saying to them:

> *'Men of Galilee, why do you stand looking up towards*
> *heaven?'* (Acts 1.11)

It brought them back to earth. You can't spend your life
staring into the space where you last saw someone. You

have to move on – they had to move on but the irony is that that meant returning to Jerusalem. In Luke's Gospel, before the account of the ascension, Jesus says to the disciples:

'Stay here in the city until you have been clothed with power from on high.' (Luke 24.49)

They were not to leave Jerusalem, not to leave the city. It was a call to stability, a call to presence. And so they go back to the room in the city that has served as their base. The tradition is that this is the Upper Room, in Luke's words, the 'room upstairs', the place in which they had shared in the Last Supper, the room into which Jesus had come after his resurrection, the room of doubt for Thomas, the room of encounter, the room in which the Lord has 'stayed with them'.

And in this space, which has become the first church, they gather again and Luke lists who is there. The list includes the women, the list includes Mary. I have called it the 'first church', the place of Eucharist, the place of presence and the house of prayer, and it is to that they devote themselves, with Mary, in expectation.

Each of our churches, wherever they are, be they large or small, cathedrals or parish churches, chapels, grand or simple, are places of Eucharist, of presence, of prayer, places of expectation and encounter. And we, gathered with Mary the mother of Jesus, wait in real time for the promise to be fulfilled, and we stay, we are faithful, we have 'stabilitas'.

This is something about which St Benedict writes:

When [the new member] is to be received, he comes be-fore the whole community in the oratory and promises stability, fidelity to monastic life, and obedience.[27]

St Benedict, in thinking about how good community is established, is concerned for the notion of community stability or, in Latin, *stabilitas loci*. In a time when the pressure is to move on – in our job, in our housing, in our attitudes, in how we live – the reminder that we also need *stabilitas loci* is an important one. Things do move on but we have to know how to balance that with the concept of stability, of staying in the place. The church is a visible sign of *stabilitas loci* and perhaps we need to be living signs of it to.

> Risen Lord,
> may I have the courage
> to stop
> to stay
> to commit
> to pause
> and not always
> to rush on
> to the next thing
> the next place
> the next person
> but to wait
> for you
> with you.
> Amen.

Pentecost

8.ooam

Birth

When the day of Pentecost had come, they were all together in one place. And suddenly from heaven there came a sound like the rush of a violent wind, and it filled the entire house where they were sitting. Divided tongues, as of fire, appeared among them, and a tongue rested on each of them. All of them were filled with the Holy Spirit and began to speak in other languages, as the Spirit gave them ability. (Acts 2.1–4)

It was the fiftieth day and the Passover was long past and they were into another celebration – Pentecost. But they were still in that same room. For the last ten days life had been different. For forty days Jesus had been around; he was with them, they felt close to him. Then, when they came back from the Mount of Olives after his ascension, they came back to this room and stayed together in prayer.

But they felt empty. Something was lacking, Jesus was lacking. They had each other, but somehow that wasn't enough.

The Sabbath was over, a new day had begun, the first day of the week, and every first day they remembered that first day when life was changed and Mary came back to the room to say that Jesus was alive, that day when Jesus had appeared among them. It was the first day yet again, a day of new beginnings, a day of new creation.

And just as they began this new day, God explodes into their lives. The windows were blown open and the force of it took their breath away. The room was filled with flame, life-giving flame, and they were each illuminated by it. Wind and flame, wind and flame – God exploding into their lives – tongues of fire, tongues of speech.

> The world is charged with the grandeur of God.
> It will flame out, like shining from shook foil;
> It gathers to a greatness, like the ooze of oil
> Crushed.[28]

The locked room becomes the scene into which God's grandeur, of which the poet Gerard Manley Hopkins speaks in the poem of that name, charges the atmosphere, flames out 'like shining from shook foil'. God disturbs them in the locked space that had become their refuge, had become their home. He needed them to get out of the room and into the rest of the world, and only wind and flame would do it. The womb must be a comfortable place for the unborn child but birth is a messy, painful, explosive moment as the child emerges into a bright, cold, harsh, demanding world, and the first thing that we want to hear is a cry, the lungs bellowing after release.

This is the birth of the church. Forced from the womb-like comfort of the Upper Room, the apostles are blown out into the world and their voice sounds in a new way like the voice of the newborn child. Their tongues are loosed and they speak, they cry, they are born, and there is no going back.

> Bring me to birth, Lord;
> bring your church to new birth, Lord.
> Where we are content with the comfort of the familiar,
> challenge us with the new
> and with wind and flame
> send us into your world
> to cry with a new voice
> and to tell the world
> the Good News of Jesus.
> Amen.

8.30am

With one voice

Now there were devout Jews from every nation under heaven living in Jerusalem. And at this sound the crowd gathered and was bewildered, because each one heard them speaking in the native language of each. Amazed and astonished, they asked, 'Are not all these who are speaking Galileans? And how is it that we hear, each of us, in our own native language? Parthians, Medes, Elamites, and residents of Mesopotamia, Judea and Cappadocia, Pontus and Asia, Phrygia and Pamphylia, Egypt and the parts of Libya belonging to Cyrene, and visitors from Rome, both Jews and proselytes, Cretans and Arabs – in our own languages we hear them speaking about God's deeds of power.' All were amazed and perplexed, saying to one another, 'What does this mean?' But others sneered and said, 'They are filled with new wine.' (Acts 2.5–13)

It's always a challenge to read this passage on this Sunday; this list of names, some familiar to us, some unfamiliar, some almost unpronounceable. Was someone taking notes, taking a roll call of the crowds gathered there? 'Where are you from?' But however the list came about, it is fascinating and exciting. This was a multicultural, diverse community. They were united by their common faith – they were all Jews – but they were from a huge variety of places and they spoke many different languages.

There are many in society who are not excited by diverse community, who find it a threat or a challenge. Any difference is too much for them – the colour of 'their' skin, the language 'they' speak, the traditions to which 'they' hold, even the food 'they' eat. The fear of the other and the despising of the other is a frightening part of our modern culture and finds its way into our politics. And we should have nothing to do with it, because God has nothing to do with it.

The glory of Pentecost is the diversity of this moment and the real reminder to us that the church does speak in every language. One of the positive outcomes of the Reformation was the release from the practices of the past to embrace the vernacular, to speak in the language understood by the people. It took many centuries for the whole of the Western Church to embrace this principle, but now that we have, who could imagine the church behaving in a different way. Each hears the gospel in their own language. And this is not just about formal language – liturgy and preaching in English or French or Shona or Mandarin or whatever it is. It is the church finding the right way of speaking, the right register in which to tell about 'God's deeds of power'. When we fail to speak so that others hear and understand then we are not the church of Pentecost.

God, who on the day of Pentecost
gave to the apostles the gift to speak
and be understood;
give to us that same gift
that we may so speak
that others will hear
and understand
and tell others
of your deeds of power.
Amen.

9.00am

In real time

But Peter, standing with the eleven, raised his voice and addressed them: 'Men of Judea and all who live in Jerusalem, let this be known to you, and listen to what I say. Indeed, these are not drunk, as you suppose, for it is only nine o'clock in the morning. No, this is what was spoken through the prophet Joel:
    "In the last days it will be, God declares,
    that I will pour out my Spirit upon all flesh,
    and your sons and your daughters shall prophesy,
    and your young men shall see visions,
    and your old men shall dream dreams."'
(Acts 2.14–17)

It was still only nine o'clock in the morning. But God doesn't hang around. God gets on with it. We began this journey on the way to Jerusalem, accompanying Jesus and his disciples on the road, through the gates of Jerusalem, to the cross, to the empty tomb and then to the mount of ascension, and today to the street outside the room in which they had been for too long locked.

This all happened in 'real time'.

God still works in real time – that is partly what the incarnation is about – God entering time, your time, my time, and making it divine time. In terms of eternity, now is but the twinkling of an eye. But God does not exist only in that eternal, timeless time, in the broad brush of for ever. The kingdom of God is about now time, our time, and we are given real time in which to know God and work for the bringing in, the full realization of what the kingdom means.

Peter is quoting the prophet Joel, as with his new-found voice he addresses the crowd. No, he is not drunk, well not in their terms, but he is 'inebriated in the Spirit', he has drunk deeply of God and as a new wine-skin holds the new wine of the kingdom. So he quotes Joel and says:

> *'Your sons and your daughters shall prophesy,*
> *and your young men shall see visions,*
> *and your old men shall dream dreams.'*

This is what we are called to do in our real time – to have the vision and the dreams and the prophetic insight that sees the possibility and the reality of God in everything around us. The clock is always ticking, but we have time, God's time, to make the passion, death, resurrection and glory of Jesus real for every person, real for them and real for us.

> May my today and tomorrow
> be your time, Lord,
> and may each moment be spent
> in making you known.
> Amen.

> And the grace of our Lord Jesus Christ and the love of God and the fellowship of the Holy Spirit be with us all evermore. Amen.

Notes and Acknowledgements

Where prayers are not attributed they are the work of the author.

All biblical quotations are from the NRSV Anglicized Edition, copyright © 1989, 1995 National Council of the Churches of Christ in the United States of America. Used by permission. All rights reserved worldwide.

1 M. L. McClure, ed., and C. L. Feltoe, trans., *The Pilgrimage of Etheria*, London: SPCK, 1919, https://www.ccel.org/m/mcclure/etheria/etheria.htm (accessed 25.6.21).
2 *Common Worship: Times and Seasons*, London: Church House Publishing, 2006, p. 271 (hereafter *Common Worship: TS*).
3 *Common Worship: Daily Prayer*, London: Church House Publishing, 2011, p. 346 (hereafter *Common Worship: DP*).
4 *Common Worship: Services and Prayers for the Church of England* (Main Volume), London: Church House Publishing, 2000, p. 79 (hereafter *Common Worship: MV*).
5 www.catholicdoors.com/prayers/english5/p03054.htm (accessed 25.6.21).
6 *Common Worship: MV*, p. 73.
7 *Common Worship: MV*, p. 407.
8 Andrew Lloyd Webber, 'Those Canaan Days', in *Joseph and his Amazing Technicolor Dreamcoat*.
9 *Common Worship: DP*, p. 345.
10 *Common Worship: DP*, p. 399.
11 William Golding, *Lord of the Flies*, London: Faber and Faber, 2004.
12 Paul Gerhardt, 1607–76, 'O Sacred Head, Sore Wounded', trans. Robert Bridges, 1844–1930.

13 Charles William Everest, 1814–77, 'Take up thy cross, the Saviour said'.

14 *Common Worship: MV*, p. 422.

15 *Common Worship*, p. 357.

16 Jacopone, da Todi, *Stabat Mater*, trans. Edward Caswall.

17 *Common Worship: MV*, p. 179.

18 *Common Worship: DP*, p. 347.

19 Henry Scott Holland, from the sermon 'Death the King of Terrors', delivered in May 1910, following the death of King Edward VI.

20 Henri Nouwen, *With Burning Hearts*, London: Orbis Books, 2016.

21 *Common Worship: Additional Collects*, London: Church House Publishing, 2017, Easter 2.

22 *Common Worship: MV*, p. 180.

23 'We have a gospel to proclaim' © words used by permission of Edward J. Burns.

24 *Common Worship: MV*, p. 401.

25 *Common Worship: Additional Collects*, Easter Day.

26 *Common Worship: MV*, p. 403.

27 The Rule of St Benedict, 58, https://christdesert.org/prayer/rule-of-st-benedict/chapter-58-the-procedure-for-receiving-brothers/.

28 Gerard Manley Hopkins, 'The Grandeur of God'.